THE

ULFILLED
FAMILY

THE

FULFILLED FAMILY

God's Design for Your Family

JOHN MACARTHUR

THOMAS NELSON
Since 1798

NASHVILLE   DALLAS   MEXICO CITY   RIO DE JANEIRO   BEIJING

Published in Nashville, Tennessee, by Thomas Nelson. Thomas Nelson is a registered trademark of Thomas Nelson, Inc.

Thomas Nelson, Inc. titles may be purchased in bulk for educational, business, fund-raising, or sales promotional use. For information, please e-mail SpecialMarkets@ThomasNelson.com.

Published in association with the literary agency of Wolgemuth & Associates, Inc.

Unless otherwise indicated, Scripture is taken from The New King James Version. © 1979, 1980, 1982 by Thomas Nelson, Inc. Used by permission. All rights reserved.

Scriptures marked KJV are from the King James Version of the Bible.

Edited by Phillip R. Johnson

Library of Congress Cataloging-in-Publication Data

MacArthur, John, 1939–
    The fulfilled family : God's design for your family / John MacArthur.
        p. cm.
    Includes bibliographical references.
    ISBN 978-0-7852-6254-1 (hardcover)
    ISBN 978-1-400280-445 (trade paper)
    1. Marriage—Biblical teaching. 2. Family—Biblical teaching. 3. Bible. N.T.
Ephesians V, 21–VI, 4—Criticism, interpretation, etc. I. Title.
BS2655.M34M34 2005
248.4—dc22   2005008268

Printed in the United States of America

08 09 10 11 12 LSI 5 4 3 2 1

To my own dear family,
especially my beloved Patricia.
"Her worth is far above rubies."

(PROVERBS 31:10)

CONTENTS

CONTENTS

INTRODUCTION

I have been speaking and writing about God's design for the family since the earliest days of my ministry. A series of sermons I preached many years ago on Ephesians 5–6, carefully examining what Scripture teaches about the roles of parents and children, has for three decades stood alone as the single best-selling set of tapes and CDs our ministry has ever produced. I first published a book on the family more than two decades ago.[1] That book was so well received that the publisher followed it up with a four-part film and video series a few years later.[2] A decade or so after that, I wrote another book and produced a new video series on Christian parenting.[3] Over the years we've published several other study guides and parenting manuals to provide practical help on family issues. Parents have devoured those resources and asked for more.

Meanwhile, in the church I have pastored for more than thirty-five years, people who were just entering the youth group when I arrived are now becoming grandparents. They, like their own parents and grandparents, want to see each successive generation of their families resist the powerful cultural trends that are steadily eroding what remains of our society's commitment to the family. And so I have been prevailed upon to address the issue of the family from a biblical perspective in writing yet again—this time in a simple handbook that distills the heart of what Scripture teaches about this most essential of all earthly institutions.

According to the Bible, God Himself ordained the family as the basic building block of human society, because He deemed it "not good that man should be alone" (Gen. 2:18). That verse stands out starkly in the biblical Creation narrative, because as Scripture describes the successive days of the Creation week, the text punctuates each stage of Creation with the words "God saw that *it was good*" (Gen. 1:4, 10, 12, 18, 21, 25, italics added). The goodness of creation emerges as the main theme of Genesis 1, and the statement "God saw that it was good" is repeated again and again, like the refrain after each stanza of a lengthy song. Then finally, after the sixth day of Creation, we're told with emphasis, "God saw *everything* that He had made, and *indeed* it was *very* good" (v. 31, italics added).

But then Genesis 2:18 takes us back to the end of day six and reveals that just before God ended His creative work, just one thing was left that was *"not* good." Every aspect of the entire universe was finished. Each galaxy, star, planet, rock, grain of sand, and tiny molecule was in place. God had created all the species of living things. Adam had already given "names to all cattle, to the birds of the air, and to every beast of the field" (v. 20). But one glaring unfinished aspect of Creation remained: "For Adam there was not found a helper comparable to him" (v. 20). Adam was alone, and in need of a suitable mate. Therefore God's final act of creation on day six—the crowning step that made everything in the universe *perfect*—He accomplished by forming Eve from Adam's rib. Then "He brought her to the man" (v. 22).

By that act, God established the family for all time. The Genesis narrative says, "Therefore a man shall leave his father and mother and be joined to his wife, and they shall become one flesh" (v. 24). Jesus quoted that verse in Matthew 19:5 to underscore the sanctity and permanence of marriage as an institution. A minister quotes that same verse practically every time he unites two believers in a Christian marriage ceremony. It is a reminder that God ordained marriage and the family, and therefore they are sacred in His sight.

So it is no mere accident of history that family relationships have always been the very nucleus of all human civilization. According to Scripture, that is precisely the way God designed it to be. And therefore, if the family crumbles as an institution, all of civilization *will* ultimately crumble along with it.

Over the past few generations, we have seen that destructive process taking place before our eyes. It seems contemporary secular society has declared war on the family. Casual sex is expected. Divorce is epidemic. Marriage itself is in decline, as multitudes of men and women have decided it's preferable to live together without making a covenant or formally constituting a family. Abortion is a worldwide plague. Juvenile delinquency is rampant, and many parents have deliberately abandoned their roles of authority in the family. On the other hand, child abuse in many forms is escalating. Modern and postmodern philosophies have attacked the traditional roles of men and women within the family. Special-interest groups and even government agencies seem bent on the dissolution of the traditional family, advocating the normalization of homosexuality, same-sex "marriage," and (in some cultures nowadays) sterilization programs. Divorce has been made easy, tax laws penalize marriage, and government welfare rewards childbirth outside of wedlock. All those trends (and many more like them) are direct attacks on the sanctity of the family.

These days, whenever families are portrayed in films, television dramas, or sitcoms, they are almost always caricatured as grossly dysfunctional. Someone recently pointed out that the only television "family" who regularly attend church together are the Simpsons—and they are cartoon exaggerations deliberately saddled with the worst imaginable traits, designed mainly to mock and malign both church and family. It's no joke, though. A relentless parade of similarly dysfunctional assortments of people assaults us on television and in the movies. Hollywood has given a broad new meaning to the word *family.*

Meanwhile, traditional nuclear families with a strong, reliable father and a mother whose priorities are in the home have been banished from popular culture, made to feel as if *they* were the caricature.

Although many Christian leaders have been passionately voicing concerns about the dissolution of the family for decades, things have grown steadily worse, not better, in society at large. Secular social commentators have lately begun to claim that the traditional nuclear family is no longer even "realistic." An article published not long ago by the online magazine *Salon* said this: "The 'ideal' American family—a father and a mother, bound to each other by legal marriage, raising children bound to them by biology—is a stubborn relic, a national symbol that has yet to be retired as threadbare and somewhat unrealistic."[4] The nuclear family simply won't work in twenty-first-century society, according to many of these self-styled "experts."

I *know* those voices are wrong, however, because I have witnessed literally thousands of parents in our church who have put into practice what the Bible teaches about the family, and they and their families have been greatly blessed for it.

As society continues its mad quest to eliminate the family, and as our whole culture therefore unravels more and more, it becomes more important than ever for Christians to understand what the Bible teaches about the family, and to put it into practice in their homes. It may well be that the example we set before the world through strong homes and healthy families will in the long run be one of the most powerful, attractive, and living proofs that when the Bible speaks, it speaks with the authority of the God who created us—and whose design for the family is perfect.

What the Bible teaches about the family is simple, straightforward, and clearly outlined in a few brief verses in Ephesians 5–6. So a study of that passage will be the basis of this book.

Almost every time I have ever spoken or written on the family, I have been drawn back to Ephesians 5:22–6:4. It is the pivotal biblical passage on the subject. It deals with every key relationship within the home. It carefully sets forth the basic dynamics of the family as God designed it to be. And through the pen of the apostle Paul, the Holy Spirit gives us a wonderful digest of God's most important standards for managing life and relationships within any household. It's a fairly short passage, but it is rich with simple truth, showing how to have a spiritually fulfilled and fulfilling family. So we'll let that brief passage be our road map as we look at what God's Word says about this vital theme.

THE FAMILY

The apostle Paul's discourse on marriage and the family in Ephesians 5 follows immediately a lengthy section instructing Christians how to walk the walk of faith. Believers in Christ should not walk the way unbelieving Gentiles walk, he said (Eph. 4:17).

He used the language of changing clothes to describe the transformation he longed to see in the Ephesians: "Put off, concerning your former conduct, the old man which grows corrupt according to the deceitful lusts, and be renewed in the spirit of your mind, and . . . put on the new man which was created according to God, in true righteousness and holiness" (vv. 22–24).

Paul listed several specific sins that characterize a life of unbelief: lying (v. 25), anger (v. 26), stealing (v. 28), evil speech (v. 29), and several wrong attitudes (v. 31). He urged the Ephesians to lay those things aside and replace them with kindness, tenderheartedness, and love. Then, at the beginning of Ephesians 5, Paul summed up what he was saying with these words: "Therefore be imitators of God as dear children. And walk in love, as Christ also has loved us and given Himself for us, an offering and a sacrifice to God for a sweet-smelling aroma" (vv. 1–2).

1

THE FIRST PRINCIPLE FOR FAMILY HARMONY:
Mutual Submission

It is vital to understand that Paul wrote his instructions about marriage in Ephesians 5 for Christians. He addressed the entire epistle to a church. The first four chapters are all about the Christian's position in Christ, and everything Paul said to fathers, mothers, and children presupposed that he was speaking to believers. If you're not a Christian, there is no hope whatsoever that you can make your marriage and your family everything God intended them to be, unless you first acknowledge your need for Christ and trust Him as Lord and Savior.

Obviously, there are non-Christian families that *appear* to be successful, to a point. They may have orderly homes, with well-behaved children and close, lasting relationships between family members. But wherever Christ is not recognized as Lord of the family, the seeds of that family's ultimate breakdown are already present. Such a family has no real *spiritual* stability, and (especially in a society where the family is already under siege) that family is courting disaster. To borrow imagery from Matthew 7:26–27, such a family is like an impressive structure built on sand. When the floodwaters come, its fall will be great.

After all, since God demands to be worshiped with a whole heart (Deut. 6:5), and He is the one who created humanity, instituted marriage, and designed the family, it is folly to imagine that our families can be what He intended if we refuse to set Him first in the family. Scripture furthermore says, "Whoever denies the Son does not have the Father either; he who acknowledges the Son has the Father also" (1 John 2:23). Jesus Himself said, "I am the way, the truth, and the life. No one comes to the Father except through Me" (John 14:6). And 2 John 9 says, "Whoever . . . does not abide in the doctrine of Christ does not have God." So the family without Christ has no firm spiritual foundation.

Besides, apart from a knowledge of the Lord Jesus Christ, we have no motivation for righteousness, no constraint from evil, and no real ability to obey from the heart what God commands for our families. That, then, is the essential foundation: Christ must be first in our hearts and in our families.

Remember, by the way, that Jesus said, "He who loves father or mother more than Me is not worthy of Me. And he who loves son or daughter more than Me is not worthy of Me" (Matt. 10:37). So He *demands* to be first in the family. It's only when we love Him more than family that we can really love our families in the highest, purest sense.

If you're not a believer, you need to acknowledge your need of the Savior. Confessing that you have sinned against God, repent, and call on the Lord Jesus Christ for salvation. Scripture says, "Whoever calls on the name of the LORD shall be saved" (Rom. 10:13).

DIVINE POWER FOR OBEDIENCE

Of course, many Christians who know and love the Lord Jesus Christ do not live consistently in accordance with His principles for the family. Why? Because they are not filled with the Spirit. That is the issue Paul addressed in the first twenty-one verses of Ephesians 5.

The first half of the chapter is about how Christians ought to walk. *Walk in love,* he said in verse 2. And then he rebuked every kind of counterfeit love: fornication, which is a corruption of marital love; uncleanness, which is an illicit love of evil; and covetousness, or the love of money and material things (v. 3). He also denounced the love of worldly companionship by admonishing the Ephesians against filthiness, foolish talking, and coarse jesting (v. 4). He said that all such worldly corruptions of love provoke God's holy wrath (v. 6).

Therefore, *walk in light,* Paul said in verses 8–14. He commanded believers to walk in accordance with "all goodness, righteousness, and truth" (v. 9) and to shun fellowship with "the unfruitful works of darkness" (v. 11). In other words, this is a call to holy living and righteous thinking. Stay in the light of the truth. Walk there, where the path is well lighted and bright.

And then, *walk in wisdom,* he said in verses 15–17. Be circumspect (v. 15). Recognize the peculiar dangers of the times in which we live, and apply yourself diligently to understanding the will of God (vv. 16–17).

All those ideas are summed up perfectly and punctuated by the simple principle of verses 18–21: *walk in the Spirit.* In other words, let the Spirit of God control you and direct your every step. It's one thing to be a believer and therefore possess the Spirit of God. It's another thing to be possessed by Him so that He controls every aspect of our walk. As Paul said in Galatians 5:25, "If we live in the Spirit, let us also walk in the Spirit."

Here in Ephesians 5, Paul made a negative parallel between being Spirit-filled and being full of wine. "Do not be drunk with wine, in which is dissipation; but be filled with the Spirit" (v. 18). Paul was not suggesting that we can possess the Spirit in varying measures. The Holy Spirit is an indivisible person—one of the divine persons of the Trinity, which means that He Himself is God—and He either indwells a person or not. No one has the Spirit of God in partial measure. But to be *"filled* with the Spirit" is to be *controlled* by the Spirit.

The contrast Paul made proves the point. To be drunk with wine is to have your faculties controlled by alcohol—

to be so given over to its influence that the wine governs you in a negative way. To be filled with the Spirit is simply to be controlled by Him so that His power dominates you in a positive way.

In other words, the Spirit of God is the one who empowers us to live lives of obedience to God. In fact, He is the *only* source of power that enables us to be subject to God's law. Without His power, we cannot even begin to please God or truly obey Him with pure motives or from a sincere heart. In Romans 8:7–8, Paul expressly said so: "The carnal mind is enmity against God; for it is not subject to the law of God, nor indeed can be. So then, those who are in the flesh cannot please God."

By contrast, those who walk in the Spirit and are controlled by Him bear the manifold fruit of the Spirit: "love, joy, peace, longsuffering, kindness, goodness, faithfulness, gentleness, self-control" (Gal. 5:22–23). Those qualities, of course, read like a recipe for healthy relationships—and especially a healthy family. So it's no wonder that Paul moved immediately from the idea of being filled with the Spirit to an extended discussion of how the family ought to function.

But notice how the transition from one subject to the

next took place. Paul first described the Spirit-filled life in these terms: "Be filled with the Spirit, speaking to one another in psalms and hymns and spiritual songs, singing and making melody in your heart to the Lord, giving thanks always for all things to God the Father in the name of our Lord Jesus Christ, submitting to one another in the fear of God" (Eph. 5:18–21). In other words, *submission* is the single principle that sums up the character of a truly Spirit-filled person. It is the key and the capstone of the Spirit's work in our hearts.

The subject of submission is what launched the apostle Paul into his message about the family.

Grace for Humility

Scripture frequently calls Christians to be humble and submissive people. Here Paul suggested that the Spirit-filled life is not a fight for the top; it's a fight for the bottom. That's exactly what Jesus taught too: "If anyone desires to be first, he shall be last of all and servant of all" (Mark 9:35). "Everyone who exalts himself will be humbled, and he who humbles himself will be exalted" (Luke 18:14).

In a community of believers, then, the principle of submission governs all relationships. Every individual submits to all others. That is the very situation Paul described in Ephesians 5:21: "submitting to one another in the fear of God." Peter said the same thing in 1 Peter 5:5–6:

> Yes, all of you be submissive to one another, and be clothed with humility, for "God resists the proud, but gives grace to the humble." Therefore humble yourselves under the mighty hand of God, that He may exalt you in due time.

The Greek word translated "submit" is *hupotasso* (from two words: *hupo*, "under," and *tasso*, "to line up, to get in order, or to be arranged"). It speaks of ranking oneself beneath another. As Christians, this is the mentality that should govern *all* our relationships: "In lowliness of mind let each esteem others better than himself. Let each of you look out not only for his own interests, but also for the interests of others" (Phil. 2:3–4).

After all, that was the example our Lord set for us. He refused to consider equality with God a thing to grasp. He stepped from heaven into this world, making Himself of no reputation, coming in the form of a lowly human—like a bondservant—even submitting to a shameful death on the cross on behalf of others (Phil. 2:5–8). In doing so, He gave us an example of how we ought to walk (1 Peter 2:21).

That is why we are to be submissive in all our relationships with one another. That is at the core of truly Christlike character, and it is also the single most important principle governing all personal relationships for all Christians. Christians are supposed to submit to one another.

Don't misunderstand or misapply that principle. It doesn't abolish the need for leadership or the principle of authority. It certainly doesn't eliminate official positions of oversight in structured institutions. In the church, for example, pastors and elders fill a God-given role of leadership, and the Bible instructs church members to submit to their elders' spiritual leadership in the life and context of the church (Heb. 13:17). Likewise within the family, parents have a clear, God-given duty to exercise authority and give guidance and instruction to their children, and children have a reciprocal duty to honor and obey their parents (Ex. 20:12; Prov. 1:8).

In fact, as Scripture plainly teaches, "there is no authority except from God, and the authorities that exist are appointed by God. Therefore whoever resists the authority resists the ordinance of God, and those who resist will bring judgment on themselves" (Rom. 13:1–2). So the principle of mutual submission isn't meant as a prescription for absolute egalitarianism. It certainly does not mean that no one is supposed to be in charge in the church, the government, or the family.

Common sense affirms the need for authority structures in human society. Of course, the largest of all social structures is a nation. Every legitimate nation *must* have a government. No nation could function without authority. God Himself designed society to function under governments. That's why both Romans 13 and 1 Peter 2:13–17 remind us that God ordained governmental authority. Rulers, kings, governors, soldiers, policemen, and judges are all necessary "for the punishment of evildoers and for the praise of those who do good" (1 Peter 2:14). Without them, there would be anarchy, and no society can survive anarchy.

Likewise, even in the smallest of human institutions—the family—the same principle applies. A family cannot survive anarchy. Someone must be responsible for discipline, direction, and spiritual leadership. Scripture recognizes this, too, as we'll see when we delve further into Ephesians 5 and 6.

Nonetheless, when it comes to one-on-one interpersonal relationships within all those institutions, the principle of mutual submission must govern how each of us treats one another. Even the person in a position of authority must be Christlike in his or her dealings with all others—which, of course, still means esteeming others better than self. Again, Christ Himself is the model for what that kind of leadership looks like. "For even the Son of Man did not come to be served, but to serve, and to give His life a ransom for many" (Mark 10:45).

Mutual submission is the principle, then, that Ephesians 5:21 spells out: "submitting to one another in the fear of God." To illustrate and further explain how the principle of submission is supposed to work in the framework of institutions where God has ordained authorities for leadership, Paul turned to the most fundamental of all human institutions, the family.

He *could* have illustrated authority and submission by explaining how the principle applies to human government. In fact, Paul did that very thing in Romans 13, and Peter did it in 1 Peter 2:13–16. He might also have explained the principle of submission by showing how it works in the context of the church. He did that in 1 Timothy 2 and 3. But here Paul's subject was *mutual* submission, so he used the family—the smallest and most intimate of all human institutions—to demonstrate how mutual submission is supposed to work on a personal and individual level, without obliterating the need for the God-ordained authority that governs every human institution.

A Good Rule of Thumb
for the Family

It is obvious that the apostle Paul never imagined for a moment that the principle of mutual submission would overthrow the very idea of authority, because as he outlined the various roles in the family, he made it very clear that the husband is the head of the home and parents have a proper and absolutely essential role of authority over children.

Nonetheless, it is vital to notice that Paul began with the principle of mutual submission. That was his theme, and it was the fundamental principle that lay beneath everything else he said about the family. If you wanted one simple rule of thumb that would do more than anything else to ensure harmony and health in the family, it would be hard to think of anything more profound or more profitable than the simple command Paul used as a springboard into his extended discussion of family roles: "[Submit] to one another in the fear of God."

Wives have often borne the brunt of Ephesians 5, as if this passage were all about the wife's subservience and the husband's dominance in the home. I have heard of more than one home where an overzealous, authoritarian husband constantly held verse 22 ("Wives, submit to your own husbands") over the wife's head. The verse might as well be carved into a baseball bat and hung over the kitchen sink.

But that kind of attitude is a violation of the whole spirit of the passage. It's interesting to note that in the Greek text, the word for "submit" doesn't even appear in verse 22. The idea is certainly implied, but the Greek expression is elliptical, omitting the word *submission*, and relying on the force of verse 21 to make the meaning clear. In other words, a literal translation of verses 21–22 would read something like this: "Submit to one another in the fear of God. Wives, to your own husbands, as to the Lord."

So keep in mind that Paul's stress was first and foremost

on the *mutuality* of submission. Everyone in the church is to submit to everyone else. The command to submit is not for wives only, but for husbands too. And verses 22–24 simply explain *how* wives are to submit to their husbands: with the same kind of respect and devotion that they owe to Christ.

But if that's the command Scripture gives to wives, does the principle of mutual submission *really* mean that the husband must submit to the wife as well? It certainly does. Paul went on to say in verses 25–29 that the husband owes the wife the same kind of love and devotion Christ showed for the church: "just as Christ also loved the church and gave Himself for her" (v. 25). There is no greater act of submission than to die for someone, and that is precisely what Christ did for the church. Since husbands are commanded to love their wives the way Christ loved the church, this requires the ultimate self-sacrifice of submission and service on the wife's behalf.

This does not mean, of course, that the husband is supposed to abdicate his God-ordained role of leadership and authority in the home. What it *does* mean is that the way he must exercise his leadership is not by lording it over his wife and family, but by serving them and sacrificing himself for them with a Christlike humility. He is to support his wife by helping bear her burdens and shoulder all her cares, even if it means sacrificing his own desires to meet her needs. It's a different kind of submission—not submission to authority per se, but a loving willingness to sacrifice for her, serve her, and seek *her* good. In other words, the godly husband's main aim must be to please his wife rather than merely doing his own will and demanding that she get in line.

Paul also went on to suggest that there's even a true sense in which the godly father must submit to his own children. Again, the father must do this not by abdicating his parental authority, but rather through sacrificial, unselfish service rendered for his children. In other words, he patterns his leadership after the example of Christ, whose meekness the prophets foretold:

> He will not quarrel nor cry out,
> Nor will anyone hear His voice in the streets.
> A bruised reed He will not break,
> And smoking flax He will not quench,
> Till He sends forth justice to victory. (Matt. 12:19–20)

Here's how Paul said a father ought to show submission to his own children: "Fathers, do not provoke your children to wrath, but bring them up in the training and admonition of the Lord" (Eph. 6:4).

Of course, Paul also commanded children to obey their parents and servants to obey their masters. But he never envisioned submission as a one-way street. Like parents, masters must also show respect and kindness to their servants (6:9).

In sum, everyone in the household has a duty to submit at some point and in some specific way to everyone else. Yes, wives must submit to the leadership of their husbands. But husbands also must bow to the needs of their wives. Certainly children need to obey their parents. But parents also have a duty to serve and sacrifice for their children. Of course servants need to yield to the authority of their masters. But masters also are commanded to treat their servants with dignity and respect—esteeming even the lowliest servant better than themselves.

In other words, Paul commanded each Christian to be an example of submission and service to all others. That simple principle is the key to harmony and happiness in the home. Domineering men who try to use Ephesians 5 as a club to keep their wives in a kind of servile submission have missed the whole point of the passage. Even if God has given you a position of leadership, you have a duty to submit and take the role of a servant—because that is precisely what Christ did for us.

Our Lord was very clear in His teaching on this matter. Matthew 20:25–27 records how Jesus called the disciples together and taught them this very lesson:

> You know that the rulers of the Gentiles lord it over them, and those who are great exercise authority over them. Yet it shall not be so among you; but whoever desires to become great among you, let him be your servant. And whoever desires to be first among you, let him be your slave.

A Helpful Perspective for Married Couples

Marriage itself is founded on the principle of mutuality. Don't imagine for a moment that the husband's God-ordained headship relegates the wife to some secondary status or destroys the essential oneness of the marriage relationship. Marriage is a partnership, not a private fiefdom for dominant husbands. That truth is woven into everything Scripture teaches about the principles of marriage and the husband's headship.

In the first place, Scripture makes it perfectly clear that men and women are spiritual equals in the sight of God. They have an equal standing in Christ and equal spiritual privileges, because we are all united with Him in the same way. Galatians 3:28 says, "There is neither Jew nor Greek, there is neither slave nor free, there is neither male nor female; for you are all one in Christ Jesus." There is no second-class spiritual citizenship. In Christ and before God, there's only oneness. We are equal. Men are not spiritually superior to women.

It's nonetheless true (and perfectly obvious) that both Scripture and nature assign different roles and different functions to men and women. The Bible is quite clear in assigning headship in every family to the husband, not the wife (Eph. 5:23). The responsibilities of teaching and leading the church are given to men, not women (1 Tim. 2:12). But women are uniquely and exclusively equipped to bear and nurture young children, and the fulfillment of that role assures that they can never be relegated to any second-class status. (I believe that is precisely what 1 Timothy 2:15 means.) Men are, as a rule, physically stronger (1 Peter 3:7 refers to the wife as "the weaker vessel"). Men are therefore responsible to carry the weight and the brunt of labor in order to provide for and protect the family. Scripture teaches that God designed the physical differences and the functional differences between men and women for a purpose—and that is why God clearly distinguishes the roles and responsibilities of husbands and wives.

Remember, however, that while their *roles* are clearly different, the *spiritual standing* of men and women in Christ is perfectly equal. Even the biblical language of two becoming one flesh underscores the essential oneness of husband and wife in a way that rules out the very notion of inequality.

In fact, the way Scripture describes the husband's role as head of his wife underscores the essential spiritual equality of men and women. In 1 Corinthians 11:3, Paul wrote, "I want you to know that the head of every man is Christ, the head of woman is man, and the head of Christ is God."

Notice several significant truths that emerge from that

one simple verse. First, God has given every husband a clear responsibility for spiritual leadership, and men dare not abdicate that duty. The husband, not the wife, is to be head of the family. That is God's design. Within every home, someone must ultimately have the responsibility of leadership, and Scripture unambiguously assigns that duty to men, not women.

Second, the model for the husband's headship is Christ. Christlike headship involves not only authority for spiritual leadership, but also the duties of care, nurture, protection, and self-sacrifice. In the words of Ephesians 5:28–29, "Husbands ought to love their own wives as their own bodies; he who loves his wife loves himself. For no one ever hated his own flesh, but nourishes and cherishes it, just as the Lord does the church." That text demolishes any notion that the husband's headship makes him in any way superior to the wife.

But third, notice the statement that comes at the end of 1 Corinthians 11:3: "The head of Christ is God." In other words, even within the Trinity, one person is head. God the Father is head over Christ.

Aren't all the persons of the Trinity fully God, and perfectly equal in essence? Of course. Jesus said, "I and My Father are one" (John 10:30). He said, "He who has seen Me has seen the Father" (John 14:9). Christ "is the image of the invisible God" (Col. 1:15). "In Him dwells all the fullness of the Godhead bodily" (Col. 2:9). There is no inequality whatsoever among the persons of the Trinity.

But there are nonetheless differences in function. The Son willingly submits to the Father's headship. The same Jesus who said, "All authority has been given to Me in heaven and on earth" (Matt. 28:18) also said, "My food is to do the will of Him who sent Me" (John 4:34). He said, "I do not seek My own will but the will of the Father who sent Me" (John 5:30). And "I have come down from heaven, not to do My own will, but the will of Him who sent Me" (John 6:38). In other words, although Father and Son are the same in essence and equally God, they function in different roles. By God's own design, the Son submits to the Father's headship. The Son's role is by no means a *lesser* role; merely a *different* one. Christ is in no sense inferior to His Father, even though He willingly submits to the Father's headship.

The same is true in marriage. Wives are in no way inferior to husbands, even though God has assigned husbands and wives different roles. The two are one flesh. They are absolutely equal in essence. Although the woman takes the place of submission to the headship of the man, God commands the man to recognize the essential equality of his wife and love her as his own body.

All of this beautifully illustrates the principle of mutual submission. And it is further illustrated by what Scripture teaches about the physical union of husband and wife. In 1 Corinthians 7:3, Paul wrote: "Let the husband render to his wife the affection due her, and likewise also the wife to her husband." He clearly recognized that each member of the marriage union has a duty to the other, and he commanded them both to fulfill that duty. But he also expressly stated that each partner has a kind of authority over the other's body: "The wife does not have authority over her own body, but the husband does. And likewise the husband does not have authority over his own body, but the wife does" (v. 4). Again, we see that each must submit to the other. That same principle of mutual submission is built into every aspect of the marital relationship, beginning with the physical union.

Once again, none of that negates what Scripture plainly

teaches about the husband's headship. But it does demonstrate clearly that the man's headship is not a kind of dictatorship where the rest of the family exists just to do his will.

In other words, the God-ordained roles in the family have nothing to do with superiority or inferiority. Many wives are frankly smarter, wiser, better educated, more disciplined, or more discerning than their husbands. God has nevertheless ordered the family so that the man is the head, because the wife is the "weaker vessel" (1 Peter 3:7) and the husband therefore owes his wife self-sacrifice and protection. The wife is *not* thereby relegated to an inferior role; she is, rather, a joint heir, who shares in all the mutual richness of the marriage.

Above all, the husband as head and the wife as weaker vessel must practice *mutual submission,* where each esteems the other as better than (never inferior to) self. The principle of mutual submission also permeates both family and church, so that in some sense every family member, as well as every Christian, should "be kindly affectionate to one another with brotherly love, in honor giving preference to one another" (Rom. 12:10).

That is the essential starting point for everything Paul had to say about the family. The rest of his teaching—in which he outlined the distinctive roles of husbands, wives, and children—is therefore set in the context of this all-important lesson about Spirit-filled humility. This one essential precept therefore establishes the bedrock principles of mutual submission, spiritual equality, tender self-sacrifice, godly humility, and loving service. Those are the keys to family harmony, and everything that comes afterward is simply an explanation of the ideal family environment—the foundation for building a true home.

THE WIFE

There's a beautiful equilibrium in the way God has designed the family to function. Husband and wife are one. Men may have the role and responsibility of spiritual headship, but in many ways, the woman has the most powerful and lasting influence in the lives of family members.

If you want to see vivid proof of this, watch just about any football game on television. Notice when the camera zooms in for a close-up of some player on the sidelines after a memorable play, he will inevitably say, "Hi, Mom!" It happens every time. I've never seen one say, "Hi, Dad!" Those great hulking brutes know the power of their mothers' *influence. Their fathers are probably the ones who taught them how to block and tackle, but it was Mom who had her hand around their hearts.*

God didn't merely relegate women to an insignificant role of subservience; He designed them to bear and nurture children, so that mothers endear themselves to children and influence the family in a way no father ever could.

That, I'm convinced, is what 1 Timothy 2:11–15 means. Paul forbade women to teach or have authority over men in the church (v. 12). Yet he acknowledged the power of their role in the home, saying, "Nevertheless she will be saved in childbearing if they continue in faith, love, and holiness, with self-control" (v. 15). He obviously could not have meant that childbirth is the way of spiritual salvation or redemption from sin for women. That would violate the clear biblical truth that we are saved by grace through faith alone (Eph. 2:8–9). What Paul meant is that women are saved from insignificance and frustration by their role in the home and the family. God has given them a powerful influence that equals and in many ways exceeds the impact of the husband's headship.

2

THE WIFE'S ROLE:
Submission, Not Slavery

How can we submit to one another in the context of a family, while still recognizing the God-ordained roles of headship and authority? That is the subject Paul turned to next, starting in Ephesians 5:22. Remember, he came to the idea of submission because that's what epitomizes the character of the person who is truly Spirit-filled. Then he outlined how mutual submission should work in a family.

The apostle's instructions for family life cover several verses, starting with Ephesians 5:22 and going through verse 4 of chapter 6. He was writing under the Holy Spirit's guidance, of course, so this was not merely the apostle's private opinion (2 Peter 1:20–21). God Himself inspired the very words of the text (2 Tim. 3:16). Paul spoke here to wives, husbands, children, and parents, in that order.

The admonition to wives is simple, covering just three verses: "Wives, submit to your own husbands, as to the Lord. For the husband is head of the wife, as also Christ is head of the church; and He is the Savior of the body. Therefore, just as the church is subject to Christ, so let the wives be to their own husbands in everything" (Eph. 5:22–24).

Several key ideas in that text are worth pointing out immediately. First, as we noted in the previous chapter, the word translated "submit" doesn't actually appear in the Greek text of verse 22. The idea is clearly implied, however, from the command of verse 21, which instructs all believers to submit to one another. Remember, wives aren't being singled out and consigned to a second-rate status. There's a sense in which *everyone* in the church must submit to everyone else (see also 1 Peter 5:5). Ephesians 5:22 simply begins a practical explanation of how *wives* ought to show their submission.

Second, notice that Paul started and ended this short section by specifying *whom* wives should submit to: "their own husbands" (v. 24). Women as a group are not made serfs to men in general, and men aren't automatically elevated to a ruling class over all women. But Scripture calls each woman to submit in particular to her own husband's headship. In other words, the family itself is the primary arena in which a godly woman is to cultivate and demonstrate the attitude of humility, service, and sacrifice called for in verse 21.

Third, the command is general and sweeping. It's not limited to wives whose husbands are fulfilling *their* function. It's not addressed only to wives with children, wives of church leaders, or even wives whose husbands are faithful believers. It's categorical and unconditional: *wives.* Anyone who fits that classification is obligated to obey the command of this verse by submitting to her own husband.

What, precisely, does this command require? We already saw in the previous chapter that the Greek word for "submit" *(hupotasso)* means "to line up under." It has the idea of placing oneself in a rank lower than someone else. This is the very idea of humility, meekness, and lowliness of mind called for in Philippians 2:3: "Let each esteem others better than himself." In no way does it imply any essential inferiority. Nor does it demote the wife to a second-class status in the home or marriage. It speaks of a functional ranking, not an inferiority of essence.

Notice also that the word *submit* is not the word *obey.* What it calls for is an active, deliberate, loving, intelligent devotion to the husband's noble aspirations and ambitions. It does *not* demand blind, fawning, slavish kowtowing to his every whim. The Greek word for "obey" would be *hupakouo,* and that is what Paul demanded of children in 6:1 and slaves in 6:5. But a wife is neither a child nor a slave, waiting on her husband while he sits in an easy chair and issues commands ("Hand me the remote!" "Get me something to drink!" "Fix me a snack!" "Fetch my slippers!" "Go to the store for me, will ya?"). Marriage is a much more personal and intimate relationship than that. It's a union, a partnership, a singular mutual devotion, and that truth is emphasized by the words "your *own* husband."

The expression itself suggests a tender partnership and mutual belonging to one another. Why wouldn't a wife *willingly* respond in submission to one whom she possesses? Paul was subtly pointing out the reasonableness and the desirability of the wife's submission to her husband.

This is a role that God Himself ordained for wives. In Genesis 3:16, God said to Eve, "Your desire shall be for your husband, and he shall rule over you." On the one hand, marriage is the perfect union of two people who become one flesh (Gen. 2:24). On the other hand, God has clearly ordained that the husband should be head in that relationship. Even nature seems to affirm the proper order. Men normally have the advantage of greater physical and emotional strength, while women usually have a more tenderhearted strength and character that equip them to be a support and encouragement—helpers suitable to their husbands.

We find a parallel passage in Colossians 3:18, where Paul also instructed wives to submit to their own husbands. But there he added a brief phrase that sheds light on why this command is so important: "Wives, submit to your own husbands, *as is fitting in the Lord*" (italics added). The word translated "fitting" means "seemly, proper, or right." It is an expression commonly used of something that is legally or morally binding. Paul seems to be pointing out that the headship of the husband and the submission of the wife are an accepted law of virtually all human society. (That has certainly been the case in most societies for the vast majority of human history, and it was most definitely true in Paul's time.) Paul was suggesting that it is "fitting"—and recognized as such throughout the history of human culture—*because* it is the divine order. It is "fitting in the Lord." This is a very strong expression about the propriety of the husband's headship.

I realize, of course, that the husband's headship and the wife's submission are not popular notions these days. Even in some Christian circles there are movements attempting to overthrow the biblical order and substitute something that is more politically correct. The world wants a more humanistic and egalitarian approach to society: a sexless, classless, artificial equality. Instead of rejecting that philosophy and upholding biblical principles, many in the church have fallen prey to the lies of our age.

But Scripture is both clear and consistent. Every time the Bible speaks about the role of the wife, the emphasis is exactly the same. This is not some chauvinistic private opinion of the apostle Paul, as some have suggested. Nor is it an unclear or ambiguous principle that's only vaguely suggested in Scripture. Every Scripture that touches on the subject of the wife's role says essentially the same thing.

1 PETER 3:1–2

The apostle Peter said it like this: "Wives . . . be submissive to your own husbands, that even if some do not obey the word, they, without a word, may be won by the conduct of their wives, when they observe your chaste conduct accompanied by fear" (1 Peter 3:1–2).

Peter employed the same word as Paul for the verb "be submissive" *(hupotasso)*. He likewise had the same emphasis on mutual belonging ("your own husbands"). Notice, also, that Peter specifically addressed situations where the husband may not even be a believer. This is therefore a key passage of Scripture, answering a question counselors commonly hear.

Often a woman will say, "Look, you don't know my husband. He is not even a Christian; he himself does not obey God. How can I submit to such a man?" But that type of situation is precisely what this verse deals with: "Even if some do not obey the word," Peter said, *submit anyway.* There is no exemption for wives who are married to unbelieving husbands. In fact, far from making such wives an exception to the rule, Peter used them as an example of what godly submission can accomplish in a marriage. He said a godly wife's submission may be the best way to win an unbelieving husband.

A believing wife *by her submission* can have a more powerful influence on her unbelieving husband than she ever will by nagging or sermonizing. By her conduct, Peter said, she may win him to Christ "without a word" (v. 1). What kind of conduct? "Chaste conduct accompanied by fear" (v. 2). Purity of life coupled with deep respect (a kind of reverential "fear") for the husband: that is how a godly wife shows submission.

Notice also the corollary: "Do not let your adornment be merely outward—arranging the hair, wearing gold, or putting on fine apparel" (v. 3). Peter's words could not be more timely today. Women shaped by contemporary society's values tend to be obsessed with external adornment. That is not where a woman's priorities should be focused, Peter said. Paul said something similar in 1 Timothy 2:9–10: "Women [should] adorn themselves in modest apparel, with propriety and moderation, not with braided hair or gold or pearls or costly clothing, but, which is proper for women professing godliness, with good works."

Don't misunderstand what this means. The apostles were not completely forbidding jewelry, stylish hair, or other feminine adornments; they were simply saying those things are not what is most important. The way a woman looks is not the measure of her true beauty.

Scripture never forbids women to adorn themselves with jewelry, makeup, or fine clothing (see also Gen. 24:22; Prov. 25:12; Song 1:10; Ezek. 16:11–13). Still, Scripture *does* plainly teach that women should not be preoccupied with external adornment. The wife who merely wants to call everyone's attention to the way she looks is actually showing a lack of submission to her own husband.

Instead, Peter said, women first of all need to cultivate inner beauty. They should be primarily concerned with "the hidden person of the heart, with the incorruptible beauty of a gentle and quiet spirit, which is very precious in the sight of God" (1 Peter 3:4). It's hard to imagine anything Peter might have said that would be more out of step with twenty-first-century notions of political correctness! He was saying that women ought to be gentle and quiet and submissive, not loud and boisterous and pushy. They ought to be concerned with their own character, and not with the world's fashion.

In other words, the real attractiveness of a godly woman—and her true strength—is that she is supportive of her husband and submissive to him, and she shows that submission through gentleness and serene stillness. That may not play well in a feminist culture, but it is what the Bible says.

Peter certainly wasn't teaching that women must blindly follow everything their husbands say—as if they could never offer a contrary opinion or think for themselves. But he was suggesting that a godly woman will seek to "win" her husband by quiet, gentle, respectful means—not by rebelling against him or by trying to take over his place as head of the family.

Notice, by the way, "the incorruptible beauty of a gentle and quiet spirit . . . is very precious *in the sight of God*" (italics added). When God looks at a woman, the external adornment of jewelry, hairdo, and makeup is not what He notices. It's the inner beauty of her character that is precious in His sight. That is what God values. That is what pleases Him. Her meekness and quietness are of priceless worth in His sight. Remember, "the LORD does not see as man sees; for man looks at the outward appearance, but the LORD looks at the heart" (1 Sam. 16:7).

Peter then set all of this in biblical and historical perspective: "For in this manner, in former times, the holy women who trusted in God also adorned themselves, being submissive to their own husbands, as Sarah obeyed Abraham, calling him lord, whose daughters you are if you do good and are not afraid with any terror" (1 Peter 3:5–6). Peter was not making any new rule. And regardless of what modern notions of political correctness might suggest, these aren't outmoded principles, either. Holiness is what godly women—women who have "trusted in God"—have always been most concerned with. They are more concerned with adorning their character than with decorating their outward appearance.

The example Peter gave is Sarah. Notice that she *obeyed Abraham, calling him lord*" (italics added). "Lord" is not merely a term of function, but an expression of deep respect. It was evidence of Sarah's meek and quiet spirit.

According to Galatians 3:7 and Romans 4:11, Abraham is the spiritual father of the faithful. According to 1 Peter 3:6, Sarah is likewise the mother of the submissive—"whose daughters you are if you do good and are not afraid with any terror."

Some women say, "I'm afraid to submit to my husband. I might lose my rights. He'll walk all over me." Peter's point is that holy women in former times "trusted in God" (v. 5), so they had no fear of obeying Him. If their husbands tried to exploit their submission, the wives trusted God to deal with the problem (see also Rom. 12:19). They knew God would honor their obedience, so they were fearless in their submission.

Notice the interesting relationship between verse 2 ("when they observe your chaste conduct accompanied by fear") and verse 6 ("if you do good and are not afraid with any terror"). There are two kinds of fear. One (v. 2) is a deep, reverential respect that is perfectly compatible with a gentle and quiet spirit. The other (v. 6) is a fear that produces terror. Genuine faith produces one kind of fear and does away with the other.

So this, according to the apostle Peter, is the character of a godly wife: she is submissive, modest, gentle, quiet, respectful, trusting, and chaste in all her conduct. That's a comprehensive description of the incorruptible feminine beauty that's so precious in God's sight. It's a good overview and starting point, but Scripture still has more to say about the role of the godly wife and mother.

TITUS 2:3–5

Now we turn to a different passage of Scripture that includes an even more detailed catalog of the duties of a godly wife. Titus 2 begins with Paul's admonition to Titus regarding "the things which are proper for sound doctrine" (v. 1). But the matters Paul went on to enumerate are not dry, abstract, or academic precepts (what many people think of as "doctrine"). Instead, Paul began with a list of things that are intensely practical, dealing with the various duties of older men, older women, young women, and young men, in that order.

Here's the section that outlines the duties of older and younger women:

> [Admonish] the older women likewise, that they be reverent in behavior, not slanderers, not given to much wine, teachers of good things—that they admonish the young women to love their husbands, to love their children, to be discreet, chaste, homemakers, good, obedient to their own husbands, that the word of God may not be blasphemed. (vv. 3–5)

The expression "older women" refers to mature women—not necessarily elderly women, but veteran wives and mothers who are already experienced at raising families and keeping a household in order. The duties Paul gave them are simple and straightforward. They are to be women of holy character ("reverent in behavior, not slanderers, not given to much wine"). And they are to be teachers ("teachers of good things").

Whom are they to teach? Younger women. What are they to teach? Paul listed a series of simple duties for wives. This section of the epistle gives a beautiful pattern for women seeking a ministry where they can put their gifts to the best use. Older women should teach younger women the skills and disciplines needed to have a successful home and marriage. Experienced wives and mothers will find their greatest avenue of ministry in teaching younger wives what they need to know to be effective wives, mothers, and homemakers.

Notice, by the way, that all the woman's biblical priorities are centered in the family and the home: "to love their husbands, to love their children, to be discreet, chaste, homemakers, good, obedient to their own husbands" (vv. 4–5).

The starting point is love—the woman's love for her own husband and children. And she expresses that love in her virtue and her self-sacrifice, chiefly in the arena of her own family home.

Although the expression "be obedient" is used in some translations of verse 5, the Greek word is not *hupakouo* ("obey"); it's the same word we encountered in Ephesians 5:22 and Colossians 3:18, *hupotasso*—"submit." Notice also, again, the idea of mutual possession: "obedient to their own husbands." The language stresses the intimacy and the mutuality of a married couple's love—and therefore self-sacrifice—for each other. Paul was in no way making the wife's submission to her husband a one-way street.

One expression in Titus 2 deserves special notice. It is the word *homemakers*. The Greek word is *oikourgous*, which literally means "workers at home." *Oikos* is the Greek word for "home," and *ergon* means "work, employment." It suggests that a married woman's first duty is to her own family, in her own household. Managing her own home should be her primary employment, her first task, her most important job, and her true career. I am convinced the Holy Spirit meant for believers to apply this even in the twenty-first century.

We have a serious problem in contemporary society: no one is home. Recent statistics from the Department of Labor show that about two-thirds of American mothers with children under age six work outside the home. Some fifty million moms are employed outside the home, and millions of preschool-age children are growing up in day-care centers rather than in the home.[1] More and more mothers have been entering the workforce since the early 1970s. And the effects are already apparent across a broad spectrum of society. The exodus of mothers from the home has surely contributed to the rising tide of juvenile delinquency, the dramatic increase in adultery and in the divorce rate, and a host of other problems related to the disintegration of the family.

Of course I'm aware of all the economic and sociological arguments people have set forth in favor of working mothers. Those arguments are frankly not very persuasive in light of the obvious detrimental effects of so many absentee mothers in today's society. But more important, the Word of God stands squarely against the modern feminist agenda when it comes to the issue of working mothers. According to the Bible, a mother's life belongs in the home. That's where her first, most important, God-given responsibility lies. That is precisely what older women are supposed to teach younger women.

In 1 Timothy 5, Paul addressed the question of a church's duty to care for widows. Rather than sending widows into the workplace to fend for themselves, Paul said each widow's extended family has a duty to provide for her (1 Tim. 5:8). In the absence of anyone who can do that, it is the church's duty to care for the widow (v. 16). In the midst of that discussion, Paul added this: "I desire that the younger widows marry, bear children, manage the house, give no opportunity to the adversary to speak reproachfully" (v. 14). There the expression "manage the house" is a translation of the Greek word *oikodespoteo*, which speaks of guiding, governing, or managing a household. Not to do so is to bring reproach on the Christian woman. This is so much God's design for women that Paul even urged young widows to pursue remarriage rather than a career. Consistently, Scripture suggests the wife's role is to work inside, not outside, the home.

This principle is germane to the idea of being submissive to "your own husband," because if you are a wife who has a career outside the home, in all likelihood, you're in circumstances that require you to be submissive to someone besides your own husband.

Remember the principle of 1 Timothy 2:15 ("[Women] will be saved in childbearing if they continue in faith, love, and holiness, with self-control"). God meant for women to wield their primary influence in the home, in the lives of their own children, and under the headship of their own husbands. Wives and mothers who opt for other career options risk forfeiting the blessing of God on their homes and families.

Does that mean women must squelch whatever gifts and talents God has given them and become domestic slaves? After all, that's the feminist caricature of the stay-at-home mom. But it's not at all how Scripture depicts the virtuous wife and mother.

PROVERBS 31:10–31

Proverbs 31 portrays the ideal woman for us. She's creative, industrious, intelligent, resourceful, and enterprising. There's nothing drab or monotonous or suffocating about her career as a wife and mother. Here is one amazing woman:

10 Who can find a virtuous wife?
    For her worth is far above rubies.

11 The heart of her husband safely trusts her;
    So he will have no lack of gain.

12 She does him good and not evil
    All the days of her life.

13 She seeks wool and flax,
    And willingly works with her hands.

14 She is like the merchant ships,
    She brings her food from afar.

15 She also rises while it is yet night,
    And provides food for her household,
    And a portion for her maidservants.

16 She considers a field and buys it;
    From her profits she plants a vineyard.

17 She girds herself with strength,
    And strengthens her arms.

18 She perceives that her merchandise is good,
    And her lamp does not go out by night.

19 She stretches out her hands to the distaff,
    And her hand holds the spindle.

20 She extends her hand to the poor,
  Yes, she reaches out her hands to the needy.

21 She is not afraid of snow for her household,
  For all her household is clothed with scarlet.

22 She makes tapestry for herself;
  Her clothing is fine linen and purple.

23 Her husband is known in the gates,
  When he sits among the elders of the land.

24 She makes linen garments and sells them,
  And supplies sashes for the merchants.

25 Strength and honor are her clothing;
  She shall rejoice in time to come.

26 She opens her mouth with wisdom,
  And on her tongue is the law of kindness.

27 She watches over the ways of her household,
  And does not eat the bread of idleness.

28 Her children rise up and call her blessed;
  Her husband also, and he praises her:

29 "Many daughters have done well,
  But you excel them all."

30 Charm is deceitful and beauty is passing,
  But a woman who fears the LORD, she shall be praised.

31 Give her of the fruit of her hands,

And let her own works praise her in the gates.

This passage is the definitive biblical answer to those who claim women are automatically stifled in their God-given role as homemakers.

Notice that the passage begins by acknowledging the rarity of such a virtuous woman. Her worth is unsurpassed (v. 10). But in no way is she repressed or enslaved to tedium because of her domestic responsibilities. She is quite literally a homemaker: a positive, constructive force in the home and family.

She is trustworthy. Her husband can trust her with the checkbook (v. 11). He has no fear that she will squander the family's resources. She is not only frugal, but she is also devoted for life to her husband's welfare (v. 12).

On top of that, she is industrious and resourceful, working with her own hands (v. 13). This is her hobby. This is her joy. This is what she loves to do. The expression literally means that she derives joy from doing handiwork for her family.

And far from being imprisoned by her domestic duties,

"she is like the merchant ships" (v. 14), seeking out bargains wherever they may be found. She'll go wherever she has to go to get the best price and the highest-quality produce or materials. She shops for "wool and flax"—raw materials. These are what she puts on the spindle and distaff (v. 19) to make thread. And with the thread, she makes tapestries and clothing (v. 22).

She sacrifices a great deal for her family, rising up early to prepare meals for them (v. 15). In other words, she cares more for them than for her own comfort. She's not lazy. She is disciplined and diligent.

Not only that, but she is shrewd in business. Having managed the household finances well and frugally, she finds a field that is a good bargain, buys the field, purchases vines, and plants a vineyard (v. 16). Now she has a home business. She is strong (v. 17); she is enterprising (v. 18); she is generous (v. 20); and she is confident (v. 21). But her home is still where she has cast her anchor.

This is not your typical caricature of a housecoat-clad, barefoot housewife. She is not frail or self-indulgent; she is not materialistic or self-centered; she is not insecure or self-absorbed. She is poised and energetic. She is wise and kind in what she says (v. 26). She is vigilant over her household and industrious for its welfare (v. 27). She is one of the main reasons for her husband's success and good reputation (v. 23).

But here's the real prize: "Her children rise up and call her blessed; her husband also, and he praises her" (v. 28). That's what fulfills her life and satisfies her heart. There's no way such a woman would ever feel trapped in a dull and dreary existence. After all, those are the priorities God Himself designed for every wife and mother. The truth is, no wife or mother can ever honestly be called "blessed" or be truly fulfilled if she sacrifices home and family for the sake of a career in any enterprise outside the home.

All of that is wrapped up in what Paul meant when he urged wives to be subject to their own husbands (Eph. 5:22). A woman in the workplace is subject to someone else's authority. Her priorities easily become confused. She is out of her element. She forfeits her highest calling.

But the home is where the truly godly woman flourishes. It's where she finds her greatest joy. And it's where she has her most important influence.

THE HUSBAND

Ask the typical man on the street to give one word that embodies the essence of headship, and he'll probably suggest words such as authority, control, power, *or* leadership. *Scripture answers the question with a different word:* love. *Certainly, headship involves a vital measure of leadership too. But it is Christlike leadership, driven by love and always tempered by a deep, tender affection. The man who rules by sheer power is a tyrant, not a head.*

"Headship" in Scripture never means raw authority. Instead, the biblical idea of headship puts the stress on sacrifice and service. The truly Christlike head will protect,

provide for, and even die for those under his headship. "Head" is not a position of superiority; it's a loving, nurturing relationship, best epitomized by Christ when He took the servant's role to wash His own disciples' feet.

The husband who imagines that God ordered the family so that his wife would be at his beck and call has it exactly backward. His role is to love and serve her. Likewise, the father who thinks children are his personal possessions and under his command hasn't begun to understand his duty as head of the family. His headship is all about his sacrifice, service, protection, and provision for them, and if he sees it any other way, he is not being Christlike in his headship.

3

THE HUSBAND'S DUTY:
Love

God divinely ordered marriage as a picture of Christ and the church. The wife's submission to the husband is designed as a living illustration of the church's submission to her Lord. That is precisely the reason Paul gave for commanding wives to submit: "For the husband is head of the wife, as also Christ is head of the church; and He is the Savior of the body. Therefore, just as the church is subject to Christ, so let the wives be to their own husbands in everything" (Eph. 5:23–24).

The husband, conversely, is supposed to be a living illustration of Christ, who "loved the church and *gave Himself* for her" (v. 25, italics added). Notice that the stress is entirely on Christ's sacrifice and service for the good of the church:

> That He might sanctify and cleanse her with the washing of water by the word, that He might present her to Himself a glorious church, not having spot or wrinkle or any such thing, but that she should be holy and without blemish. So husbands ought to love their own wives as their own bodies; he who loves his wife loves himself. For no one ever hated his own flesh, but nourishes and cherishes it, just as the Lord does the church. For we are members of His body, of His flesh and of His bones. "For this reason a man shall leave his father and mother and be joined to his wife, and the two shall become one flesh." This is a great mystery, but I speak concerning Christ and the church. Nevertheless let each one of you in particular so love his own wife as himself, and let the wife see that she respects her husband. (vv. 26–33)

Remember, Paul's theme in Ephesians 5 (from verse 21 on) is *mutual submission*. When he introduced the husband's headship in verse 23, he was not changing the subject. He was not saying everyone else needs to submit to the man, who as the head of the family gets to impose his will and his desires on everyone else. Not at all. Paul's whole point here was that a husband best shows Christlike headship by voluntary, loving sacrifice and service on behalf of the wife— which is as much a form of *submission* as the wife's allegiance to her husband's leadership and the children's obedience to their parents.

The sinful tendency of fallen men is to dominate their wives by brute force. Even some Christian men are guilty of being too heavy-handed with authority. They practically lord it over their wives, as if marriage were designed to be a master-slave relationship. Some have even tried to claim that Ephesians 5:24 supports such a notion, because it urges wives to be subject to their husbands "in everything." But that perspective of the husband's role is antithetical to the pattern of headship Christ gives us.

Anyone who thinks that way simply needs to read further in Ephesians 5. When Paul turned his attention to husbands, he didn't say, "Husbands, rule your wives; order them around; command them; exercise authority over them; dominate them"— or anything of the sort. He told them to love their wives as Christ loves the church: sacrificially, tenderly, meekly, and with a servant's heart. This is how husbands are to show submission to their wives.

The Meaning of Love

Authentic love is incompatible with a despotic or domineering approach to headship. When Paul commanded husbands to love their wives as Christ loved the church, he was in effect forbidding them to exercise severe or abusive authority over their wives. If the model of this love is Christ, who "did not come to be served, but to serve, and to give His life a ransom for many" (Matt. 20:28), then the husband who thinks he exists so his wife and children can serve him couldn't be farther off the mark.

It is significant, by the way, that husbands are not commanded to lead, but to *love* their wives.

Consider the implications of a *command* to love. This suggests that genuine love is not merely a feeling or an involuntary attraction. It involves a willful choice, and that is why this is in the form of an imperative. Far from being something we "fall into" by happenstance, authentic love involves a deliberate, voluntary commitment to sacrifice whatever we can for the good of the person we love.

In 1 Corinthians 13:4–8, the apostle Paul outlined the characteristics of true love. Notice that none of the features of true love are involuntary, passive, or feelings-based. In fact, Paul used active verbs wherever possible, rather than adjectives, underscoring the truth that love is both dynamic and deliberate:

> Love suffers long and is kind; love does not envy; love does not parade itself, is not puffed up; does not behave rudely, does not seek its own, is not provoked, thinks no evil; does not rejoice in iniquity, but rejoices in the truth; bears all things, believes all things, hopes all things, endures all things. Love never fails.

So when Paul commanded husbands to love their wives, he was calling for all the virtues outlined in 1 Corinthians 13, including patience, kindness, generosity, humility, meekness, thoughtfulness, liberality, gentleness, trust, goodness, truthfulness, and long-suffering. It is significant that all the properties of love stress selflessness and sacrifice. The husband who truly loves his wife simply cannot wield his authority over her like a club. Far from being overlord of the family, the godly husband and father must make himself servant of all (see also Mark 9:35).

THE MANNER OF LOVE

How, in practical terms, should a husband demonstrate his love for his wife? Remember, first of all, that the model for the husband's headship is Christ, and Christ's love for His church is therefore the perfect pattern and prototype for every husband's relationship with his wife. That elevates the husband's love for his wife to a high and holy level. The husband who abuses his role as head of the family dishonors Christ, corrupts the sacred symbolism of the marriage union, and sins directly against his own Head, Christ (1 Cor. 11:3). So the husband's duty to love his wife in a Christlike manner is of supreme importance. In effect, the husband's duty is to model the spirit of Christ for his family. No one in the family is given a greater responsibility. (It's highly significant, I think, that Paul's exhortation to husbands is the longest, most detailed section of Ephesians 5:22–6:9.)

The passage suggests four characteristics of Christlike love.

Love That Gives

Paul's whole point, of course, was that Christ's love was a self-sacrificial love. He "loved the church and *gave Himself for her*" (Eph. 5:25, italics added). Jesus Himself indicated that of all love's qualities, a willingness to sacrifice self is the greatest: "Greater love has no one than this, than to lay down one's life" (John 15:13). Authentic love is always self-sacrificial. Here is conclusive proof that the husband's headship is not to be domineering and tyrannical. The first mark of his love for his wife should be his willingness to sacrifice his own self.

The typical tyrant is arrogant and self-centered. The person who loves sacrificially is the polar opposite: humble, meek, concerned more with others than with self. Again, Christ is the model. Though He existed eternally as God and was therefore worthy of all worship and honor, He laid all that aside in order to come to earth and die for sinners. Scripture says He "made Himself of no reputation, taking the form of a bondservant, and coming in the likeness of men. And being found in appearance as a man, He humbled

Himself and became obedient to the point of death, even the death of the cross" (Phil. 2:7–8). That is what Christ's sacrificial love looked like, and that is what God calls husbands to emulate.

Remember, also, that Christ did not bestow His love for the church on people who deserved that love. As a matter of fact, they were people who deserved only wrath and condemnation. But He loved them even though they did not deserve it. "God demonstrates His own love toward us, in that while we were still sinners, Christ died for us" (Rom. 5:8).

So this kind of love does not depend on the lovableness or the attractiveness of the object. It is unconditional, unqualified, and unrestricted. Paul was not telling husbands to love their wives if the wives deserved it, or if the husbands felt like it. He was giving an absolute command. This is a reminder once again that love involves a deliberate act of the will. If love were just a tingly feeling, then when the feeling stopped, love would be dead. That's precisely what most people imagine love is like. But biblical love is a willful commitment to self-sacrifice, and it is not at all based on how we might "feel" at any point about the object of our love.

An amazing principle underlies this command, however.

What we choose to love invariably becomes extremely attractive to us. A heart determined to love sees only beauty. So authentic love naturally *results* in the passions of desire and attraction we often associate with love. Of course, the feelings can come and go, rise and fall, or be present with lesser or greater intensity from time to time. Such feelings themselves are not love and should not be confused with it. True love, once more, is the deliberate commitment of oneself to another.

That is precisely what Scripture demands of husbands: a self-giving commitment to the wife. A husband who is unwilling to sacrifice for his wife does not even know what true love is. Husbands who regard their wives as servants under their sovereign headship haven't begun to appreciate the true biblical pattern for marriage and the family. Selfish husbands therefore will never know what it is to have a fulfilled marriage and family. True happiness in marriage is possible only to those who follow the divine pattern. Sacrifice is the true way of blessing, as Jesus Himself taught: "It is more blessed to give than to receive" (Acts 20:35).

Properly understood, Ephesians 5:25 ("Husbands, love your wives, just as Christ also loved the church and gave

Himself for her") demands that the husband die to self. In effect, he is called to crucify himself for the sake of his wife. It's not talking about some petty sacrifice, such as helping his wife with the dishes every now and then. It means the husband must devote his entire life—and quite literally even be willing to die—for the good of his wife.

Remember, genuine love "does not seek its own" (1 Cor. 13:5). The man who is concerned only with getting what he can from marriage is sowing the seeds of destruction in his own family. To love your wife as Christ loved the church is to be preoccupied with what you can do for her, not vice versa. After all, Christ loves us not because of any benefit He gains, but simply and only because He is a gracious Lord who delights to bestow on us His favor.

Love That Guards

The love of a godly man for his wife is the kind of love that safeguards her purity. Paul said Christ's sacrifice for the church had this ultimate object in mind: to "sanctify and cleanse" her (Eph. 5:26)—to make her glorious, without spot or wrinkle, "that she should be holy and without blemish" (v. 27). Her purity was His primary concern.

Likewise, in marriage, it is every husband's solemn duty to guard his wife's purity. No one would ever deliberately defile someone he really loves. Remember, authentic love "does not rejoice in iniquity, but rejoices in the truth" (1 Cor. 13:6). How could a loving husband ever delight in something that compromises the purity of the one he loves?

On the contrary, the husband who loves his wife as Christ loves the church will naturally *hate* anything that defiles her. He will protect her against any threat to her virtue. He will strive to make his home a place where Christ is honored and everything that might defile is excluded. He will never knowingly lead her into any kind of sin. He won't deliberately provoke her or exasperate her so that she succumbs to anger or any other temptation. But he will guard her from anything and everything that might dishonor her, degrade her, demean her, or tempt her to sin. And he himself will be an example of purity, knowing that whatever defiles him will ultimately defile her too.

Notice the primary way Christ maintains the purity of the church: "with the washing of water by the word" (Eph. 5:26). Husbands have a duty to ensure that their wives are regularly exposed to the cleansing and purifying effect of the Word of

God. The husband is to be the spiritual leader and priestly guardian of the home. It is his duty to make sure the Word of God is at the center of the home and family. Of course he ought to lead his family in participation in a church where the Word of God is revered and obeyed. But above all, he himself needs to be devoted to the Word of God and proficient enough in handling the Scriptures that he can be the true spiritual head in the marriage (see also 1 Cor. 14:34–35).

That means the husband's priorities must be in order. If a man sits for hours, day after day, month after month, year after year, watching sports on television or otherwise neglecting his family's spiritual needs, he will eventually reap a bitter harvest. Here is where the husband's willingness to sacrifice for the good of his wife becomes intensely practical. If cultivating her sanctification and guarding her purity are not priorities over the evening television lineup, that husband is falling far short of loving his wife the way Christ loved the church.

But in the same way Christ lovingly guards the purity of His church, the godly husband will seek his wife's sanctification, purity, and spiritual growth. That is every husband's responsibility.

Love That Cares

Genuine love also involves tender care, and Paul expressed that idea this way: "Husbands ought to love their own wives as their own bodies" (Eph. 5:28).

We spend a lot of time and energy taking care of our own bodies. We exercise; we eat; we wear clothes to look nice and stay warm. When we're sick or fatigued, we rest. When our bodies hurt, we seek relief from the pain. We take care of our bodies constantly—giving them whatever food, clothing, comfort, recreation, relaxation, or rest they need. We're attentive to our own bodies, concerned with their needs, sensitive and responsive to whatever they desire.

That is the kind of love Paul commanded husbands to show their wives. Notice, once again, Scripture is not describing love only as an emotion. This sort of love is active, voluntary, dynamic—something we do, not something we passively "feel."

It's only reasonable that a man would love his wife the way he loves his own body, because in marriage, "the two . . . become one flesh" (v. 31). That is the way God designed marriage. Paul was actually quoting from Genesis 2:24, which (as we noted at the beginning of this book) describes how God first ordained marriage. In other words, this is a principle that is built into the idea of marriage itself. It applies universally, and it has been true from the beginning. Husbands ought to love their wives with the same care they give to their own bodies, because, after all, the two *are* one flesh.

This is what marriage is all about. Marriage itself is consummated with the literal bodily union of husband and wife. From that point on, the husband should regard the wife as his own flesh. If she hurts, he ought to feel the pain. If she has needs, he should embrace those needs as his own. He should seek to feel what she feels, desire what she desires, and in effect, give her the same care and consideration he gives his own body.

The apostle Peter had these words of advice for husbands: "Husbands, likewise, dwell with [your wives] with understanding, giving honor to the wife, as to the weaker vessel, and as being heirs together of the grace of life" (1 Peter 3:7). Notice several things that emerge from that text:

First, from the husband's perspective, headship is something that carries a greater *responsibility*, not necessarily a higher degree of privilege. Peter had already affirmed the divine order of the husband's headship (vv. 1–6). He recognized that the wife is "the weaker vessel." And yet he saw this as a reason for the husband to sacrifice personal privilege and "[give] honor to the wife."

Second, although the husband's duties clearly include leadership, nothing here indicates that the husband ought to regard the wife as anything other than a joint heir and partner. Husband and wife are "heirs together of the grace of life."

Third, the text suggests three practical ways husbands ought to prefer their wives over themselves:

Consideration. "Husbands . . . dwell with them with understanding" (v. 7). One of the most common complaints counselors hear from wives about their husbands is this: "He doesn't even try to understand me. He's insensitive to the way I feel."

Proper love for one's wife involves consideration for how she feels. Husbands need to be aware of the concerns their wives express, the goals they have set, the dreams they cherish, the desires that drive them, the things they fear, and the anxieties they carry. That requires a deliberate effort to see as she sees and feel what she feels. It means listening to her carefully, giving her time to share her heart, and having empathy with what she is feeling. That sort of understanding doesn't seem to come naturally to most husbands, but that is what every wife needs—and that is what Scripture demands of husbands.

Chivalry. Peter continued: "giving honor to the wife, as to the weaker vessel." It is an undeniable fact of nature that in general, women are physically weaker than men. That is what this refers to. These days, referring to women as "the weaker sex" may not seem politically correct, but in no way did Peter mean this as an insult to women. On the contrary, he brought it up as a reason for husbands to treat their wives with a gentle, loving chivalry. A husband honors his wife when he employs his strength to serve her in ways that account for her weakness. There are all kinds of practical ways to show this type of courtesy to a wife, from symbolic things like opening doors for her, to more practical things such as changing tires, washing windows, and moving furniture.

Serve your wife with your strength, Peter was saying. Acknowledge that she is the weaker vessel, and use your physical strength to serve her whenever her weakness places her at a disadvantage. This is one of the key ways husbands are to submit to their wives—by thoughtfully showing them honor in their weakness.

Communion. The final phrase of 1 Peter 3:7 puts it all in perspective: "and as being heirs together of the grace of life, that your prayers may not be hindered." Again we see that although women may be physically weaker than men, men and women are spiritual equals. Husband and wife are joint heirs of "the grace of life." By that expression, Peter was indicating that marriage itself is the best part of life—like the topping on a sundae. And husband and wife share together in that grace.

I'm thankful for my wife, Patricia. She is my best friend and closest confidant. She is also my foremost spiritual partner, with whom I share constantly the issues that we bring to God. Peter recognized the importance of that relationship and cited it as the primary reason for husbands to be considerate and chivalrous toward their wives: "that your prayers may not be hindered." If there is any kind of breach in the husband-wife relationship, in effect, it can close the windows of heaven.

So Peter urged husbands to be understanding and to

show honor and empathy to their wives. It's simply another way of saying what the apostle Paul said in Ephesians 5:28: "Husbands ought to love their own wives as their own bodies."

Returning, then, to Ephesians 5, we see that Paul went on in verse 29 to say, "No one ever hated his own flesh, but nourishes and cherishes it." That's true. There are, of course, people who *claim* they don't like themselves very much. We hear a lot these days about the problem of "low self-esteem"—which, more often than not, turns out to be just another excuse to pamper oneself with false pity.

But we don't by nature hate ourselves. It's perfectly natural to avoid what hurts us, seek what we desire, eat what we have an appetite for, and avoid whatever threatens life and limb. Our instinct for self-preservation is one of our most basic drives. Scripture recognizes that. There's nothing essentially wrong with it, and there's certainly no virtue in self-flagellation or other ascetic means of punishing one's own body.

When Scripture commands us to love our neighbor as ourselves (Mark 12:31), it tacitly recognizes how foreign self-hate is to the human heart. Jesus called that law the second greatest commandment (Matt. 22:39). And a moment's reflection will reveal that "love your neighbor as yourself" is simply the principle of mutual submission expressed in different language.

If that principle applies even to our love for our neighbors, it must apply in an infinitely more personal way to the love between husband and wife. Indeed, the language Paul used in Ephesians 5 with regard to husbands and wives seems deliberately chosen to underscore the absolute intimacy of the husband's tender love for his wife: "Husbands ought to love their own wives as their own *bodies*" (v. 28, italics added).

The terms Paul employed are strikingly warm and personal: "No one ever hated his own flesh, but *nourishes* and *cherishes* it" (v. 29, italics added). The Greek verb translated "nourishes" is a word used only here and in Ephesians 6:4, where it is translated as "bring them up"—and describes the nurture of a little child. It conveys the idea of feeding and bringing to maturity. It seems to speak not only of the husband's duty as a provider, but also his role as spiritual leader in the family.

The word translated "cherishes" literally means "to warm."

The same Greek word is used in 1 Thessalonians 2:7, where it describes how "a nursing mother cherishes her own children." It is a word that might be used to describe a nesting bird, brooding over her chicks. It's a beautiful expression, and in this context, it conveys the ideas of warmth and security, suggesting that a godly husband will tenderly shelter and defend his wife as someone fragile and precious.

A wife is a God-given treasure to be nourished and cherished—just as Christ does the church (Eph. 5:29). She is her husband's to care for; his partner and loving helper; his to fulfill every need for love, friendship, companionship, and physical intimacy. She is his to be the mother of his children. The two are one flesh. It is the most perfect and most intimate union on earth.

Paul's whole point is that marriage is a living illustration of Christ's love for the church. That's why the husband's duty to care for his wife is such a sacred responsibility, especially in a Christian marriage. The wife is not only one with the husband; she is one with Christ as well. In marriage she is one with her husband; in salvation she is one with Christ. How her husband treats her therefore reflects what he thinks of the Lord (see also Matt. 25:40). "For we are members of His body, of His flesh and of His bones" (Eph. 5:30).

Love That Lasts

Since the husband's love for his wife pictures Christ's love for the church, it must also be the kind of love that outlasts every trial and overcomes every obstacle. That, of course, was God's original design for marriage, and we are reminded of that fact by verse 31, where Paul quoted from Genesis 2:24: "For this reason a man shall leave his father and mother and be joined to his wife, and the two shall become one flesh." When Christ was questioned about divorce, He quoted that same verse, then underscored the permanence of the union: "So then, they are no longer two but one flesh. Therefore what God has joined together, let not man separate" (Matt. 19:6).

Every marriage is consummated in an earthly sense by a *physical* union: "The two shall become one flesh." Children conceived by that union will literally bear the genetic pattern of two people who have become one flesh. But marriage also involves a *spiritual* union. *God* is the one who joins husband and wife together (Matt. 19:6). Marriage is the union of two souls, so that the marriage union knits the two together in every aspect of life. Their emotions, intellects, personalities, desires, and life goals are inextricably bound together. They share every aspect of life: worship, work, and leisure. That is how God designed marriage to be.

Naturally, then, God also designed marriage to be a *permanent* union, unbroken and uncorrupted. Scripture says, "The Lord God of Israel says that He hates divorce" (Mal. 2:16). The biblical terminology of Ephesians 5:31 stresses the permanence of the marriage union: "A man shall leave his father and mother and be joined to his wife."

The Greek word translated "leave" in that verse is *kataleip.* It's an intensified verb meaning "to leave behind" or "to abandon completely." When a couple marries, each former parent-child relationship is radically severed. Married children still have a vital connection with their parents, of course. (Even adult children are commanded to honor their fathers and mothers.) But it is a whole new kind of relationship. Marriage removes the child from the parents' direct authority and establishes a completely new household with a new head—the husband. Leaving father and mother is an essential part of every marriage. When either the husband or the wife in a new marriage fails to move completely out from under the parents' umbrella both physically and emotionally, it invariably causes problems in the marriage.

The word translated "be joined to" is a Greek term *(proskolla)* that literally speaks of gluing something together. It describes a permanent, unbreakable bond. That is an apt description of God's ideal for marriage. It's a union held together by lasting love that absolutely refuses to let go.

THE MOTIVE OF LOVE

Scripture is clear: God's plan for the family begins with life-long monogamous marriage, which is grounded in sacrificial love. Why is this of such supreme importance? What is the highest and best motive for husbands to love their wives? Paul gave the answer in Ephesians 5:32: "This is a great mystery, but I speak concerning Christ and the church." In other words, the husband's love for his wife is a sacred duty because of what it illustrates.

Christ is the heavenly Bridegroom and the church is His bride (Rev. 19:7–8; 21:9). Because marriage pictures that union, the husband must be Christlike in his love for the wife, and she must be submissive to his headship. Otherwise, the divine object lesson is destroyed and the marriage cannot be what God intended it to be.

What higher motive could there be for a husband to love his wife? By loving her as Christ loved the church, he honors Christ in the most direct and graphic way. He becomes the embodiment of Christ's love to his own wife, a living example to the rest of his family, a channel of blessing to his entire household, and a powerful testimony to a watching world.

THE CHILDREN

The Old Testament law repeatedly underscores children's duty to obey their parents. God obviously wanted to make it clear that He does not regard rebellion against parents as a small matter. Under Moses' law, extreme insolence against one's own parents could be punished even by death: "For everyone who curses his father or his mother shall surely be put to death. He has cursed his father or his mother. His blood shall be upon him" (Lev. 20:9). "And he who strikes his father or his mother shall surely be put to death" (Ex. 21:15).

Plain stubbornness could also result in capital punishment in cases where a son or daughter proved utterly incorrigible:

> If a man has a stubborn and rebellious son who will not obey the voice of his father or the voice of his mother, and who, when they have chastened him, will not heed them, then his father and his mother shall take hold of him and bring him out to the elders of his city, to the gate of his city. And they shall say to the elders of his city, "This son of ours is stubborn and rebellious; he will not obey our voice; he is a glutton and a drunkard." Then all the men of his city shall stone him to death with stones; so you shall put away the evil from among you, and all Israel shall hear and fear. (Deut. 21:18–21)

Of course, that describes a worst-case scenario. It applied only to the most chronic and extreme rebels—juvenile delinquents. What we know of Israel's history suggests that it was only rarely if ever practiced (perhaps because the threat itself was an effective deterrent in most cases). It nonetheless stands in the biblical record as graphic proof that God was very serious about children's duty to honor their parents.

But Scripture also teaches that children do not naturally obey their parents. "Foolishness is bound up in the heart of a child" (Prov. 22:15). We are all born as "children of disobedience" (Eph. 2:2 KJV) with a sinful nature and a bent toward rebellion. No one needs to teach a child how to disobey or rebel. "They go astray as soon as they are born, speaking lies" (Ps. 58:3).

The only way children can learn obedience is by being taught to obey. That's what parental discipline is all about. Much of the book of Proverbs discusses this theme. "He who spares his rod hates his son, but he who loves him disciplines him promptly" (13:24). "Do not withhold correction from a child, for if you beat him with a rod, he will not die. You shall beat him with a rod, and deliver his soul from hell" (23:13–14).

That passage is describing how parents should teach their children to obey; it's not about punishing hard-core delinquents. It isn't describing any kind of abusive physical force. These days the English word beat has connotations of severe battery that causes injury. That's not what this means. The Hebrew word translated "beat" means "punish" or "smite." It speaks of something firm, but not necessarily injurious. In fact, Ezekiel 21:14 and 17 use the same word to speak of clapping the hands together.

Of course Scripture isn't prescribing any kind of punishment that would injure a little child. But it does suggest that parental discipline should be firm, even painful (see also Prov. 20:30).

Still, parents should always administer discipline with love, not in rage or with sadistic pleasure. The model for this kind of discipline is God Himself. "For whom the LORD loves He corrects, just as a father the son in whom he delights" (Prov. 3:12). But God disciplines His children only "for our profit, that we may be partakers of His holiness" (Heb. 12:10).

4

THE CHILDREN'S DUTY:
Obedience

After admonishing wives and then husbands, the apostle Paul turned his attention to children. It's the beginning of a new chapter (chapter 6) in Paul's epistle to the Ephesian church, but this is a continuation of the same subject he had been discussing. He was moving systematically through the family, describing each family member's duty, and showing what mutual submission means in the context of the family structure.

Children, of course, are to show submission by obeying their parents. This is one of only a handful of texts in Scripture that directly address children in particular (see also Ex. 20:12; Prov. 1:8–9; 6:20; Col. 3:20). Virtually every time the Word of God speaks to children, the message is the same, aptly summarized by Ephesians 6:1–3: "Children, obey your parents in the Lord, for this is right. 'Honor your father and mother,' which is the first commandment with promise: 'that it may be well with you and you may live long on the earth.'"

In verse 2, Paul was quoting the fifth commandment from Exodus 20:12: "Honor your father and your mother, that your days may be long upon the land which the LORD your God is giving you." That commandment is the turning point of the Ten Commandments. The first four commandments (often called the First Table of the Law) describe aspects of our duty to God: have no other gods; make no graven images; don't take the Lord's name in vain; and remember the Sabbath. The remaining six commandments (the Second Table of the Law) spell out our duties with respect to other people: honor your parents; do not murder; do not commit adultery; do not steal; do not bear false witness; and do not covet.

The starting place and the foundation for all earthly

relationships is the child's duty to honor his or her parents. Since that is the first relationship we ever experience, this is the first moral principle every child needs to learn. It is fitting, therefore, that the leading commandment in the Second Table of the Law governs the parent-child relationship.

As the apostle Paul pointed out, the fifth commandment is also "the first commandment with a promise." In fact, this is the only one of the Ten Commandments that comes with a promise. Two other commandments (the second and the third) are accompanied by threats. The fourth commandment is followed by an extensive explanation of the reason for the commandment. But "honor your father and your mother" is the only commandment with a benediction for those who keep it.

It's a promise of long life, blessing, and prosperity. Writing under the Holy Spirit's inspiration, Paul brought together the promise of Exodus 20:12 ("that your days may be long upon the land which the LORD your God is giving you") with the fuller language of Deuteronomy 4:40: "that it may go well with you . . . and that you may prolong your days [on the earth]"—so that there are two parts to the promise. On the one hand, it promises *quality of life* (that it may be well with you). On the other hand, it promises *length of days* (and you may live long).

The "promise" was a divine pledge to the Israelites as a *nation*. As far as individuals are concerned, this is really more of a maxim than an ironclad surety. In other words, it is a truism, not a guarantee. Some people honor their parents and die young anyway. There have undoubtedly been cases where people who have despised their parents' authority have nevertheless lived to old age. But as a general rule, the principle is true. Rebelling against parents has built-in consequences that tend to shorten one's life.

The apostle Paul's instructions to children in Ephesians 6 are notable for their straightforward simplicity. There's no long list of duties, no complex set of instructions—just one simple command: "Obey your parents." Of course, all *other* duties—such as love for God, love for brothers and sisters, love for neighbors, and all other important moral precepts—will be covered by this rule if the parents simply do what they are commanded in verse 4: "Bring them up in the training and admonition of the Lord." Children who learn how to obey their parents will thereby also learn to obey

God. This highlights once again the supreme importance of a Christian family.

Why Is Obedience So Hard to Learn?

Teaching children to obey is no easy task. It is a full-time, years-long duty for parents, often frustrating and always requiring diligence. Why is it so difficult?

Well, as we noted in the preface to this chapter, obedience comes naturally to no one. When Adam fell, he dragged the whole human race into sin (Rom. 5:12–21). That is known as the doctrine of original sin. It means that people by nature are hostile to God, utterly unable to obey God out of pure motives or from a pure heart, and therefore unable to do anything that truly pleases God (Rom. 8:7–8). All Adam's offspring are born naturally depraved and with a bent toward sin and rebellion.

So there are really two major obstacles all parents face in teaching their children to obey: not only is the world they live in corrupt, but they themselves are sinful creatures too. They face a difficult struggle both inside and outside.

Our Children Live in a Fallen World

It's an undeniable fact that the world we live in is corrupt and cursed with sin. Someone has said that more empirical evidence exists for the doctrine of original sin than for any other truth of Scripture. That's true. Although it may be difficult for some people to accept the truth that Adam's sin corrupted the entire human race, it's really impossible for a reasonable person to deny the abundance of evidence for that doctrine.

Wherever you look, the effects of human sin corrupt society. All the trends currently undermining the family (divorce, infidelity, homosexuality, delinquency, and so on) are nothing but expressions of human sinfulness. And sin is so deeply ingrained in society that it has shaped our very culture. It is impossible to live in the world and not be profoundly impacted by the corruption of sin all around.

For example, our age in particular has turned defiance into a virtue and made obedience something to be mocked. This warped and rebellious worldview comes through in every aspect of popular culture. Entertainment, music, and even newscasts glorify revolt and rebellion against every form of authority. The very culture in which children live today teaches them to rebel against authority.

Statistics show that the average child living at home in America watches at least twenty-eight hours of television each week.[1] (For some kids, the total is much higher.) Programming that targets young people is often the very *worst* at deliberately glamorizing sin. By the time most young people graduate from high school, they have been overexposed to the grossest kinds of evil through "entertainment" media in mind-numbing ways—so that nothing seems particularly appalling anymore. After all, drug use, immorality, violence, and profanity are standard fare on television. When a whole generation has been raised on a steady diet of that stuff, it's no wonder that sin no longer seems exceedingly sinful to them.

What is the predictable result? Drug abuse, violent crime, sexual promiscuity, and other forms of lawlessness are at epidemic levels among teenagers. Large, disturbing subcultures exist among young people who practice bizarre forms of body modification (such as tattooing and piercing), immerse themselves in occultism, or openly practice other forms of antisocial behavior. Who can deny that sin and rebellion have our society, and their tragic effects are most vividly apparent in the culture of our young people?

Yet millions in society—especially among those in control of the entertainment media—glory in the evil. The apostle Paul prophetically foretold times like these. He wrote to Timothy:

> Know this, that in the last days perilous times will come: For men will be lovers of themselves, lovers of money, boasters, proud, blasphemers, *disobedient to parents,* unthankful, unholy, unloving, unforgiving, slanderers, without self-control, brutal, despisers of good, traitors, headstrong, haughty, lovers of pleasure rather than lovers of God, having a form of godliness but denying its power. And from such people turn away! (2 Tim. 3:1–5, italics added)

It's fitting that rebellion against parents is at the heart of that list of evils, because virtually all the other sins listed (especially self-love, thanklessness, a lack of self-control, headstrong haughtiness, and hedonism) are inevitable fruits of youthful rebellion against parents. A culture of rebellion breeds every other kind of sin as well.

And that is why we are living in an age of moral anarchy. That is the culture in which our children are growing up. Although the wise parent will minimize a child's exposure to the evils in the world, there's simply no way to isolate our children completely from all those influences. Even if we could, that would not erase all the challenges we face as parents. There's still that other major reason our kids find rebellion easy and obedience difficult.

Our Children Are Fallen Creatures

The reason all the corruption of this world poses such a danger to children is that they themselves are fallen creatures and are therefore naturally drawn to evil. Job 5:7 says, "Man is born to trouble, as the sparks fly upward."

Children are simply prone to rebellion. Some may seem more rebellious than others, but no child is naturally obedient. Depravity is universal (Rom. 3:10–18). No one ever has to be *taught* to disobey. We're all born with that ability.

Furthermore, something in our fallen human nature makes rebellion appealing to us. No one naturally likes to obey. When we're told *not* to do something, the command itself seems to provoke a desire to do what is forbidden.

The apostle Paul recognized this and wrote in Romans 7:7–8: "I would not have known covetousness unless the law had said, 'You shall not covet.' But sin, taking opportunity by the commandment, produced in me all manner of evil desire."

Every toddler, as soon as he can scoot around, gives living proof of this principle. Tell him not to touch something, and as soon as your back is turned, he will go straight for the forbidden object. That is precisely the spirit of Adam's sin, isn't it? We inherited that tendency from him and will carry it all our lives.

That's why parents cannot afford to be fainthearted or passive. They cannot quit before the task is complete. And it's *never* complete. Often the struggle to teach children to obey only gets harder as they grow older.

Yet the command of Ephesians 6:1 applies to adolescents and young adults as long as they remain in the home and dependent on the parents for support—until they marry or establish their own households. The Greek word translated "children" in Ephesians 6:1 applies to adult offspring as well as young toddlers.

As we have seen, God's plan is for sons and daughters

who marry to leave their parents and cleave to their spouses (Gen. 2:24). Part of "leaving" means the child is no longer under the direct authority of the parents, of course. But the duty to *honor* mother and father continues (Matt. 15:3–6). That lifelong respect is the legacy of being reared to obey. And the child who learns to obey while at home will continue to obey the moral and biblical principles and honor the godly parents' values even after leaving home.

But Ephesians 6:1 speaks primarily to children still living at home and under their parents' authority. The parallel passage in Colossians 3:20 defines the extent of obedience that is required: "Children, obey your parents *in all things*" (italics added). As long as they are in their parents' custody and the parents have a responsibility to provide for them, the child's responsibility is to obey, even though obedience is the most unnatural thing to every human heart.

How Is Obedience Learned?

So how can parents teach their children to obey? First of all, positive instruction and a good example are paramount. Punishment is a last resort (though an essential one), not the starting point. Kids need positive guidance, with positive reinforcement.

Did you realize that even Jesus had to learn obedience? Hebrews 5:8 says, "He learned obedience by the things which He suffered." Born "under the law" (Gal. 4:4), He was bound by the fifth commandment to honor His father and mother, like any other child. He learned to submit to them (Luke 2:51–52).

Not that He ever *dis*obeyed or acted sinfully. He was of course "in all points tempted as we are, yet without sin" (Heb. 4:15). He remained "holy, harmless, undefiled, separate from sinners" (Heb. 7:26), even during His earthly life.

But remember that when Jesus took on human form, it was not in appearance only. He was a true man. He had all the natural, nonsinful limitations and frailties of humanity. He experienced hunger and thirst (Matt. 4:2; John 19:28). He grew weary (John 4:6). And as a child, He learned things—including obedience. His earthly parents taught Him, and He learned the lessons well.

As a matter of fact, the way Jesus learned and grew is essentially the same way every child learns and grows. Of course, because He was sinless, He did not require punishment. But He no doubt learned through *positive* instruction and reinforcement from loving parents. Scripture says He "increased in wisdom and stature, and in favor with God and men" (Luke 2:52).

Notice that He grew in four ways: intellectually ("in wisdom"), physically ("and stature"), socially ("in favor with . . . men"), and spiritually ("in favor with God"). All children have needs in those same four areas, and the wise parent will meet those needs with positive instruction and a good example.

Our kids have *intellectual needs,* because they are born without any knowledge of what is good for them and what is not. Parents need to teach them the principles of wisdom. And obedience is the first step toward wisdom.

They have *physical needs,* and the younger they are, the greater those needs. Of all the higher mammals, humans have the least strength and coordination at birth. They can't even roll over. As they grow, they gain muscle and dexterity, but in the meantime, the parents' umbrella of authority is a necessary part of the protection God has established.

They have *social needs,* because they have to learn how to interact with others. Babies are concerned with nothing but their own needs, and the only form of communication they know is crying. As they grow, they have to be taught concern for others. They have to learn to communicate rationally with others. They have to learn such things as how to share and how to have empathy for others. Learning to obey their parents is the first vital step in learning all the social skills they will need for life.

Above all, they have *spiritual needs.* Their parents need to teach them the gospel of salvation. They will not learn to love the Lord naturally. They need to be instructed about Him and hear the principles of His Word. And for children, obedience to parents is the first spiritual principle they need to understand and submit to.

In other words, the parents' authority provides a safe environment in which children can grow in all these ways. The children's obedience is the fuel for all their learning and growth, and the better they learn to obey, the more proficiently they will grow in wisdom, in stature, and in favor with God and men.

What's Involved in Obedience?

The obedience Paul called for in Ephesians 6:1 is above all an attitude, not merely visible behavior. The Greek word for "obey" is *hupakou*—from a root that means "to hear" or "to heed." It includes the idea of listening attentively as well as obeying. That is why Paul cited the fifth commandment as an exact parallel: "*Honor* your father and mother" (v. 2, italics added).

It's notable that the fifth commandment itself doesn't use the word *obey.* "Honor" is a broader concept that certainly includes the idea of obedience—but at the same time it condemns attitudes of resentment, anger, reluctance, or other forms of defiance that mechanical external obedience often masks. Obedience without honor is hypocrisy. Scripture is calling for obedience from the heart.

Paul further explained the proper attitude of obedience with the phrase at the end of verse 1: "Obey your parents *in the Lord*" (italics added). In other words, when children rightly obey, they do it as unto the Lord (see also Col. 3:23–24)—because God delegates parents' authority to them. The parents therefore are ministers of God as far as the child is concerned (see also Rom. 13:1–4).

How far does this principle extend? What if the parents are unbelievers who order their children to do what the Word of God forbids? In that case, Scripture gives a clear principle:

"We ought to obey God rather than men" (Acts 5:29). Of course, children must obey all the standard parental commands such as "Clean your room" and "Take out the trash" in every instance. Only in those rare situations when the parent orders a child to violate an explicit command of Scripture is the child permitted to refuse obedience.

Sadly, some parents do command their own children to do evil, and some even persecute their kids for Christ's sake. That is to be expected. After all, Jesus said, "I have come to 'set a man against his father, a daughter against her mother, and a daughter-in-law against her mother-in-law'; and 'a man's enemies will be those of his own household'" (Matt. 10:35–36). Because of sin and unbelief, the gospel sometimes causes bitter division in families.

I've known of cases, for example, where non-Christian parents have tried to forbid their believing children to read Scripture or have fellowship with other believers. In the most extreme instances, some parents have even tried to force their children to renounce Christ completely. When parents set themselves against Christ in that way, the child has a clear biblical duty to stand with Christ. Jesus went on to say, "He who loves father or mother more than Me is not worthy of Me" (v. 37).

But even then, the child's general attitude toward the parents must not become defiant or belligerent. If forced to disobey, the child must willingly bear the consequences. When punished for being faithful to Christ, the son or daughter should bear the reproach gladly (Matt. 5:10–12). And meanwhile, in all other matters, the child should remain obedient and continue to honor the parents in every way possible.

The *attitude* is of supreme importance. If the attitude is right, proper actions will be the natural result. "For as he thinks in his heart, so is he" (Prov. 23:7). If the actions are right but the attitude is wrong, that's nothing but hypocrisy, which dishonors the parents and disgraces the child. In our family, the children were more often disciplined for bad attitudes than bad behavior.

So the message for children is short and simple: obedience—in both attitude and action—is "right" (Eph. 6:1). It is "well pleasing to the Lord" (Col. 3:20). It is honoring to the parents. And it is good for children—protecting them from a world of evil, prolonging their lives, and bringing them an abundance of blessing.

THE PARENTS

Today's parents tend to be more passive and less involved in their children's lives than any generation in our nation's history. They have turned their children over to artificial, surrogate parents. Day-care centers, relatives, the television set, and the child's own peers often have far more influence on the moral and social development of today's children than parents do.

That is an abdication of the parents' duty before God. The Lord Himself gave parents—not schools, youth leaders, Sunday school teachers, or anyone else—the primary responsibility for the nurture and admonition of children.

And He meant for parenting to be a full-time job, with no time off.

I'm not suggesting you have to homeschool your children. In fact, you may not have the skills to teach your kids academic subjects as well as a schoolteacher. What I'm saying is that you need to remain intimately involved in every aspect of their lives, including school—regardless of what educational option you choose for your kids. Even a Christian school is not an appropriate proxy for parenting; it's only a supplement to the parents' teaching role. Parents are still the ones who have the responsibility for supervising the child's education. And they should continue to exercise careful oversight of every aspect of what their children learn, especially when someone else is doing the teaching. That's why parenting is still a full-time job, even when the children go to school.

Notice what God said to the Israelites when He gave them the Ten Commandments: "These words which I command you today shall be in your heart. You shall teach them diligently to your children, and shall talk of them when you sit in your house, when you walk by the way, when you lie down, and when you rise up" (Deut. 6:6–7).

Clearly, God meant for parenting to be a full-time, life-long occupation. Every hour of the day and every season of life is a teaching opportunity for the diligent parent. If you want to make the most of those opportunities, you can't take time off or quit before your children are grown. You certainly can't turn your kids over to others and expect them to give your children the kind of nurture and admonition only a faithful parent can provide.

5

THE PARENTS' DUTY:
Nurture and Admonition

Children have the easy role in the family. All they have to do is obey their parents. The *parents'* duty is what is really hard. They have to set a good example, be diligent teachers, give regular correction, and provide consistent discipline—all without frustrating their kids in the process.

Someone has pointed out that we spend the first twelve months of our children's lives teaching them to walk and talk, and the next twenty years trying to get them to sit down and be quiet. Parenting is not for the faint of heart. The skills and patience necessary to be good parents don't come naturally for parents any more than obedience comes naturally for children.

Remember: parents, like children, are fallen and sinful. We inherited Adam's guilt and depravity too. We were born with the same inclination toward sin our kids have. Redemption in Christ gives us a new heart and a capacity to love righteousness, but until redemption is complete, we will always struggle with the remnants of our sinful flesh, which causes us to do things we hate (Rom. 7:15–24). We still "groan within ourselves" (Rom. 8:23; see also 2 Cor. 5:2). We still face conflicts on the outside and fears on the inside (2 Cor. 7:1). And all those things still thwart our efforts to be good parents.

In other words, even though the Bible commands children to obey their parents in all things, parents are not always right. Parents are by no means infallible, and woe to parents who pretend otherwise.

As a matter of fact, the principle of mutual submission covers the parents' role too. There's a true sense in which parents must submit to their children, and Paul defined how that works in Ephesians 6:4: "You, [parents,] do not provoke your children to wrath, but bring them up in the training and admonition of the Lord."

By the way, the word translated "fathers" in most English

versions of that verse is the Greek word *patera,* which can mean either "fathers" or "parents." In Hebrews 11:23, it clearly means "parents" and is translated that way. That also seems to be the clear sense of the word in Ephesians 6:4. That is, I believe, the best way to understand the passage.

Of all the principles Paul outlined for families in Ephesians 5:22–6:4, this one was no doubt the most contrary to Paul's own culture. In the Roman world of that time, fathers presided over their families, and they could quite literally do with them whatever they pleased. A Roman law known as *patria potestas* (literally, "the father's power") gave absolute property rights over their families to all heads of households who were Roman citizens. Wives, children, and household slaves were by law the patriarch's personal possessions, and he could do with them whatever he wished. He had full authority, without resorting to any court of law, to disown his children, sell them into slavery, or even put them to death. Obviously, in the Roman world, it was the child who tried to avoid provoking the father to wrath, not vice versa.

But the apostle's instructions turned the cultural norm on its head. Even parents need to submit to children, Paul taught. And they do this by sacrificing to give their children what they need, while taking care not to exasperate or discourage them. There are three parts to the command.

DON'T PROVOKE THEM

First of all, Paul said, "do not provoke your children to wrath." Don't thoughtlessly aggravate them. Don't unnecessarily goad them. Don't deliberately exasperate them. Don't foolishly discourage them. But show your submission to them by treating them with gentleness, kindness, consideration, and respect. After all, that's an essential part of being a good example to them.

Paul was not suggesting that every time a child becomes angry, it is the parent who has sinned. Obviously, children can and do become angry apart from any sinful provocation on the parent's part.

Nor does this excuse children who get angry, regardless of the circumstances. Children have a duty to honor their parents and obey them from the heart, even when the parents are aggravating.

Nonetheless, it does suggest that parents who sin this

way are doubly guilty. Not only do they violate their duty as parents, but they also cause their own children to stumble.

The expression "provoke . . . to wrath" is one word in the Greek: *parorgiz.* It applies to every kind of anger, from silent fuming, to indignant outbursts, to full-fledged rebellious rage. Children express their wrath in different ways.

Parents provoke their children to wrath by various means too. Over my years as a pastor, I have observed many different ways parents have done this. Avoid all of them. Here are just a few examples:

Some parents crush their children with *excessive discipline.* I have known parents who seemed to think that if discipline is good for a child, extra discipline must be even better. They constantly waved the threat of corporal punishment as if they loved it. No parent should ever be eager to punish. And no punishment should ever be brutal or bullying. Parents should always administer discipline with the good of the child in mind, never more than necessary, and always with love.

Other parents provoke their children by *inconsistent discipline.* If you overlook an infraction three times and punish the child severely the fourth time, you will confuse and exasperate your child. Parental discipline must be consistent.

That's one of the main reasons parenting requires full-time diligence.

Some parents provoke their children with *unkindness.* I cringe when I hear parents deliberately saying mean-spirited things to their children. But many parents do, it seems—and to compound the problem, they often seem to do it in public. I've overheard parents saying things to their own children they would never say to anyone else. That's a sure way to crush a child's heart and provoke him to resentment.

Another way parents provoke their kids is by *showing favoritism.* Isaac favored Esau over Jacob, and Rebeka preferred Jacob over Esau (Gen. 25:28). The resentment their favoritism provoked caused a permanent split in the family (Gen. 27). But Jacob made the same mistake with his own children, showing such favoritism to his youngest, Joseph, that Joseph's brothers plotted to do away with him (Gen. 37). Although God sovereignly brought about much good from what happened to Joseph (Gen. 50:20), that doesn't change the fact that Jacob and his family had to endure much sorrow, heartache, and evil because of the chain of events that began with Jacob's favoritism.

Some parents actually goad their children to exasperation

through *overindulgence*. They are too permissive. Research from many different sources shows that children who are given too much autonomy feel insecure and unloved. No wonder. After all, Scripture says parents who let their children misbehave with no consequences are actually showing contempt for the child (Prov. 13:24). Children know that instinctively, and it exasperates them.

On the other hand, some parents frustrate their children by *overprotection*. They fence them in, suffocate them, deny them any measure of freedom or trust. That's a sure way to provoke a child to frustration: make your child despair of ever having any liberty at all unless he or she rebels.

Plenty of parents arouse their children's anger through constant *pressure to achieve*. If you never praise your kids when they succeed but always drive them to do even better next time; if you neglect to comfort and encourage them when they fail; or worst of all, if you force your children to try to fulfill goals you never accomplished, they will certainly resent it. It's fine to encourage our children to excel. In fact, that is a natural and normal part of parenting (1 Thess. 2:11). But don't forget to balance your desire to see them realize their full potential with a little patience and understanding, or you will provoke the bitterest kind of resentment.

Other ways parents provoke their children are through neglect, constant criticism, condescension, indifference, detachment, cruelty, sanctimoniousness, hypocrisy, a lack of fairness, or deliberate humiliation. All of those things provoke children to exasperation by *discouragement*. And that's precisely what Paul said in the parallel passage, Colossians 3:21: "Fathers, do not provoke your children, lest they become discouraged."

That is the negative side of Ephesians 6:4. There are two positive parental duties also given in that verse: "training and admonition." *Training* involves nurture and education (in fact, the word is translated "nurture" in the King James Version). *Admonition* involves warning, reminding, correcting, and sometimes rebuking. We'll examine each of these positive duties individually.

Nurture Them

The usual Greek word for "child" is *pais*. It's the root of the word translated "training," *paideia*. So this term speaks of child-rearing, and it encompasses several aspects: training, instruction, chastening, discipline, and nurture. In fact, the word *paideia* is translated all those ways in various English versions. (The same word appears here, once in 2 Timothy 3:16, and four times in the discussion of divine chastening in Hebrews 12:5–11.)

I like the word *nurture* because I think it captures the tenderness and affection that befit the raising of children. The context as well as the word itself show that Paul was calling for loving instruction and sympathetic care.

"Bring them up," Paul said (employing the same word translated "nourish" in Ephesians 5:29). Children cannot reach maturity by themselves. Parents have to bring them up. Children *need* strong parental guidance. In fact, the more they are left to themselves, the less they will become what they ought to be. Proverbs 29:15 says, "A child left to himself brings shame to his mother."

That, once more, is because of their natural depravity. As we saw in the previous chapter, children are born with a bent toward sin. We have already noted that this is one of the most formidable obstacles to the *child's* obedience. It is also the single greatest issue *parents* need to deal with.

In other words, parents, you cannot raise your children to be what they ought to be unless you help them realize that their most fundamental needs are spiritual—and unless you nurture your children accordingly. (Again we see the vital importance of a Christian family.)

Children have a heart problem. They are constitutionally sinful. Like their parents, and like the rest of the Adamic race, they are fallen. What they need most are regenerate hearts. This is the most fundamental issue in parenting. It's not ultimately about behavior; it's about the child's heart.

Behavior simply reflects what is in the heart. In Mark 7:21–23, Jesus said, "From within, out of the heart of men, proceed evil thoughts, adulteries, fornications, murders, thefts, covetousness, wickedness, deceit, lewdness, an evil eye, blasphemy, pride, foolishness. All these evil things come from within and defile a man." Proverbs 4:23 says, "Keep your heart with all diligence, for out of it spring the issues of life." Luke 6:45 says, "A good man out of the good treasure of his heart brings forth good; and an evil man out of the evil treasure of his heart brings forth evil. For out of the abundance of the heart his mouth speaks." Many other biblical passages teach the same thing: bad behavior stems from a corrupt heart. Therefore, it's not enough to correct our children's behavior; what they really need is heart renewal.

Parents have no power to renew a child's heart, of course. Only God can do that (Ezek. 36:26–27). But parents need to help their children understand that their hearts are desperately in need of regeneration, their real problem is sin, and *all* their greatest needs are therefore spiritual. Parents also need to direct their children to Christ as the only Savior who can provide the forgiveness and redemption they need. That is the most important of all parental duties, and the parent who neglects it is not faithfully bringing his children up "in the training and admonition of the Lord."

Naturally, children also lack maturity, and the parents' instruction should aim at giving them the experience and understanding they need as they mature. But they should do *all* such instruction in the context of addressing the root issue of the child's spiritual needs. Depravity is not a problem our kids will naturally outgrow.

In other words, it is not enough to correct wrong behavior and teach good manners. Proper parenting is not about behavior control, or even merely about teaching kids to be obedient. To bring up our children in "the training and admonition of the Lord" is to direct them to Christ.

Parents cannot guarantee their kids' salvation. We can't believe on their behalf. Only the Holy Spirit can give them new hearts (John 3:6–8). But parents must be evangelists to point the way to Christ, and they should also be vigilant and persistent prayer warriors on behalf of their children. All of that is wrapped up in "the training and admonition of the Lord."

The parents' duty extends far beyond pointing them to Christ for salvation. When the child comes to faith, that is wonderful, but parents still have much nurture and instruction to give. And the main issues are still spiritual. It's not enough to teach them social skills; we need to train them how to withstand temptation. It's not enough to teach them how to share with others and respect others' property; they also need to learn why sin is so exceedingly sinful. They need to know that sins such as pride, lust, and covetousness are an offense to God. It is the parents' duty to *teach* them—"*bring them up* in the training and admonition of the Lord" (Eph. 6:4, italics added). Don't imagine they will pick these things up by osmosis.

Parents *do* need to deal with the external behavioral issues, of course, but that is not where nurture and instruction begin and end. Kids also need to learn that the root issue is their sin, and they need to be taught the remedy for sin. Chastisement is not for the benefit of frustrated parents. It's supposed to be for the benefit of the child. And in order to get the full benefit, they need to understand that the real problem is their sin—sin that offends *God.*

By the way, if you're going to faithfully bring up your children in "the training and admonition of the Lord," you need to teach them the *whole* counsel of God. All of Scripture is profitable for them (2 Tim. 3:16), so don't neglect any of its doctrine, reproof, correction, or instruction in righteousness.

Remember that Deuteronomy 6:6–7 ("Teach [these words] diligently to your children, and . . . talk of them when you sit in your house, when you walk by the way, when you lie down, and when you rise up") makes full-time spiritual instruction the parents' primary duty. That is the kind of "nurture" our children need, and that is what Ephesians 6:4 means. Don't neglect that duty.

Admonish Them

The word translated "admonition" in Ephesians 6:4 is *nouthesia* in Greek. It means "rebuke" or "warning." It is actually a close synonym of *paideia*. Paul wasn't contrasting these two expressions; he was simply repeating and developing the concept. The process of "training" (nurture) actually *requires* "admonition" (warning, correction, exhortation, and even rebuke).

That brings up the issue of discipline. What method of punishment should parents use? Verbal rebukes? Time-outs? Grounding? Removal of privileges? Corporal punishment? All of the above?

No issue in parenting seems to confound parents more than the question of how best to discipline children. Many secular "experts" insist that all forms of physical punishment are abusive and seriously injurious to the psyche of the child. Some even claim that parents should use *no* form of negative correction with children—positive reinforcement alone is sufficient, they say.

Scripture says otherwise. In fact, the Bible prescribes corporal punishment and says it is a necessary element of parental love (Prov. 13:24; 23:13). It is by no means the *only* method of discipline Scripture recognizes, however. No single punishment is right for every child in every situation. All the forms of discipline I mentioned above—and many others—are suitable in various situations. Parents need to choose and apply whatever methods of discipline they use with wisdom, restraint, love, and understanding.

An exhaustive treatment of this issue is far beyond the scope of this little book, of course.[1] But here are three simple principles that will be helpful to parents who want to understand how to discipline their children without provoking them to anger:

First, *discipline should be consistent.* "Let your 'Yes' be 'Yes,' and your 'No,' 'No'" (Matt. 5:37). If a parent tells a child not to do something and the child does it anyway, the parent *must* correct the child. To ignore the offense is to sanction the disobedience and encourage more rebellion. Furthermore, don't be severe sometimes and lenient other times. Discipline should always be firm (not necessarily harsh) but always loving and always consistent. Be equally firm with all your children. And keep your word when you make promises.

Second, *the punishment should fit the crime.* Reserve the harshest punishments for instances where the child has willfully disobeyed. Don't punish a child who has merely been careless with the same rigor you might punish an act of overt defiance. Use corporal punishment only for the most serious infractions; don't mete it out automatically with every petty offense. The best parents are creative with their punishments, linking the punishment to the offense. A child who is unkind to a brother or sister, for example, might be punished by taking over one of the offended sibling's chores. Severe disobedience calls for a spanking.

Finally, remember that *as much of your training as possible should be positive.* Be sure you notice and reward positive behavior at least as often as you punish misbehavior. It's significant, I think, that the fifth commandment itself is reinforced with positive motivation—a promise of blessing to those who obey. Rewards for obedience are perfectly legitimate.

Those principles—like all the biblical principles for families—are simple and straightforward. Parenting isn't complex; what makes it "difficult" is failing to follow these principles faithfully, diligently, and consistently.

My prayer for you, dear reader, is that God will give you grace to see, wisdom to understand, and a firm determination to apply all the simple principles of God's Word as they pertain to your family. May your family be blessed, strengthened, and fulfilled as you put the truth of God into practice together.

ABOUT THE AUTHOR

John MacArthur, one of today's foremost Bible teachers, is the author of numerous best-selling books that have touched millions of lives. He is pastor-teacher of Grace Community Church in Sun Valley, California, and president of The Master's College and Seminary. He is also president of Grace to You, the ministry that produces the internationally syndicated radio program *Grace to You* and a host of print, audio, and Internet resources—all featuring John's popular, verse-by-verse teaching. He also authored the notes in *The MacArthur Study Bible*, which has been awarded the Gold Medallion and has sold more than 500,000 copies.

John and his wife, Patricia, have four children who have given them thirteen grandchildren.

For more details about John MacArthur and all his Bible-teaching resources, contact Grace to You at 800-55-GRACE or www.gty.org.

NOTES

Introduction

1. John MacArthur, *The Family* (Chicago: Moody, 1982).

2. John MacArthur, *How to Raise Your Family: Biblical Essentials for No-Regret Parenting* (Chicago: Moody, 1985).

3. John MacArthur, *Successful Christian Parenting* (Nashville: Word, 1998), later reissued in paperback and retitled *What the Bible Says About Parenting*.

4. Amy Benfer, "The Nuclear Family Takes a Hit," *Salon.com.*, 7 June 2001.

Chapter 2

1. U.S. Department of Labor, Alexis M. Herman, Secretary, "Meeting the Needs of Today's Workforce: Child Care Best Practices" (1998—see www.dol.gov/wb/childcare/child3.pdf), 8.

Chapter 4

1. American Academy of Child and Adolescent Psychiatry, "The Impact of Media Violence on Children and Adolescents" (www.aacap.org/training/developmentor/content/1999fall/f1999_a3.cfm).

Chapter 5

1. I've covered the subject in somewhat more detail in *Successful Christian Parenting*, 85–88; 152–56.

CPSIA information can be obtained at www.ICGtesting.com
Printed in the USA
LVOW040540270112

265828LV00001B/1/P